THE WORKING LIFE

A Renaissance Painter's Studio

A Renaissance Painter's Studio

TITLES IN THE WORKING LIFE SERIES INCLUDE:

An Actor on the Elizabethan Stage

The Cavalry During the Civil War

A Renaissance Painter's Studio

A Sweatshop During the Industrial Revolution

A Worker on the Transcontinental Railroad

THE WORKING LIFE

A Renaissance Painter's Studio

JAMES BARTER

LUCENT BOOKS®

THOMSON

™

GALE

San Diego • Detroit • New York • San Francisco • Cleveland • New Haven, Conn. • Waterville, Maine • London • Munich

THOMSON
★
GALE

Cover Image: A nineteenth-century painting by Felice Schiavoni
of Raphael in his studio painting *La Fornarina*.

© 2003 by Lucent Books. Lucent Books is an imprint of The Gale Group, Inc.,
a division of Thomson Learning, Inc.

Lucent Books® and Thomson Learning™ are trademarks used herein under license.

For more information, contact
Lucent Books
27500 Drake Rd.
Farmington Hills, MI 48331-3535
Or you can visit our Internet site at http://www.gale.com

LIBRARY OF CONGRESS CATALOGING-IN-PUBLICATION DATA

Barter, James
    A Renaissance painter's studio / by James Barter.
        p. cm. — (The working life series)
Summary: Describes the arduous training and difficult day-to-day working lives of
painters in Florence during the Renaissance and discusses how their changing approach
to the art they created elevated their standing and influence in Florentine society.
Includes bibliographical references and index.
    ISBN 1-59018-178-6 (hardback : alk.paper)
    1. Painting, Renaissance—Juvenile literature. 2. Artists' studios—Europe—History—
Juvenile literature. 3. Painters—Europe—Social conditions—History—Juvenile literature. [1. Artists—Social conditions—History. 2. Artists' studios—Italy—Florence—
History. 3. Painting, Renaissance. 4. Renaissance—Italy—Florence.] I. Title. II. Series.
    ND170 .B35 2003
    759.5'51'09024—dc21

                                                                    2002007892

Printed in the United States of America

CONTENTS

FOREWORD   8

INTRODUCTION
Renaissance Painters and Florence   10

CHAPTER ONE
The Emergence of Renaissance Painters   12

CHAPTER TWO
Education in a *Bottega*   22

CHAPTER THREE
Working in a *Bottega*   38

CHAPTER FOUR
Working Outside a *Bottega*   50

CHAPTER FIVE
Patrons and Painters   60

CHAPTER SIX
Art as a Business   72

CHAPTER SEVEN
The Private Lives and Personalities of
    Florentine Painters   85

Notes   97
For Further Reading   101
Works Consulted   102
Index   104
Picture Credits   111
About the Author   112

FOREWORD

"The strongest bond of human sympathy outside the family relations should be one uniting all working people of all nations and tongues and kindreds."

Abraham Lincoln. 1864

Work is a common activity in which almost all people engage. It is probably the most universal of human experiences, the drive to work. As Henry Ford, inventor of the Model T said, "There will never be a system invented which will do away with the necessity of work." For many people, work takes up most of their day. They spend more time with their co-workers than family and friends. And the common goals people pursue on the job may be among the first thoughts that they have in the morning, and the last that they may have at night.

While the idea of work is universal, the way it is done and who performs it varies considerably throughout history. The story of work is inextricably tied to the history of technology, the history of culture, and the history of gender and race. When the typewriter was invented, for example, it was considered the exclusive domain of men who worked as secretaries. As women workers became more accepted, the secretarial role was gradually filled by women. Finally, with the invention of the computer, the modern secretary spends little time actually typing correspondence. Files are delivered via computer, and more time is spent on other tasks than the manual typing of correspondence and business.

This is just one example of how work brings together technology, gender, and culture. Another example is the American plantation slave. The harvesting of cotton was initially so cumbersome and time consuming that even with slaves, its profitability was doubtful. With the invention of the cotton gin, however, efficiency improved, and slavery became a viable agricultural tool. It also became a Southern tradition and institution, enough that the South was willing to go to war to preserve it.

The books in Lucent's Working Life series strive to show the intermingling of work, and its reflection in culture, technology, race, and gender. Indeed, history viewed through the lens of the average worker is both enlightening and fascinating. Take the history of the typewriter, mentioned above. Readers today have access to more technology than any of their historical counterparts, and, in fact, though they would find the typewriter's keyboard familiar, they would find using it a bore. Finding out that people spent their days sitting over that machine (with no talk of carpal tunnel syndrome!) and were valued if they made no typing errors because corrections were cumbersome to make and, in some legal professions, made documents invalid, is an interesting story that involves many different aspects of history.

The desire to work is almost innate. As German socialist Ferdinand Lassalle said in the 1850s, "Workingmen we all are so far as we have the desire to make ourselves useful to human society in any way whatever." Yet each historical period offers a million different stories of the history of each job and how it was performed. And that history is the history of human society.

Each book in the Working Life series strives to tell the tale of these anonymous workers. Primary source quotes offer veracity and immediacy to each volume, letting the workers themselves tell their stories. In addition, thorough bibliographies tell students where they can find out more information and complete indexes allow for easy perusal of the text. While students learn about the work of years gone by, they gain empathy for those that toil, and, perhaps, a universal pride in taking up the work that will someday be theirs.

RENAISSANCE PAINTERS AND FLORENCE

Each year during the warm Tuscan summer months, millions of visitors converge on Florence to experience and enjoy the world's most revered collection of Renaissance art. Central to the city's collection is the finest assemblage of Renaissance paintings executed during the fifteenth and sixteenth centuries. They can be found scattered throughout the city's museums, churches, civic buildings, and stately country villas. These artistic treasures painted on canvases, wood panels, and walls were executed by the hands of revered virtuosos such as Michelangelo, Leonardo da Vinci, Botticelli, Raphael, Ghirlandaio, Giotto, and a number of lesser known yet equally impressive masters.

These world-renowned paintings, whose values today are de-scribed not in terms of millions of dollars but, rather, in the simplicity of the term *priceless,* had very real and measurable costs associated with them when they were orginally painted.

RENAISSANCE ITALY

Artists and patrons made verbal agreements and signed contracts that, among other things, specified the painter's fee. In addition to these centuries-old contracts, letters written by the creators of these treasures and their documented conversations with writers reveal fascinating insights about not only the paintings themselves but the personal lives that helped shape them.

This book provides a behind-the-scenes glimpse into the working lives of Renaissance painters. During this period, artists did not dabble at their work on the side while relying on other jobs for a steady income. Every master painter trained for years as an apprentice, called a *garzone*. They then labored long days painting to earn enough money to pay their bills—often with little left over. Understanding the daily difficulties that Renaissance painters surmounted while executing their masterpieces adds a new dimension for appreciating these paintings.

CHAPTER 1

THE EMERGENCE OF RENAISSANCE PAINTERS

Renaissance painters emerged at the crossroads of many revolutionary events to create unparalleled demands for their works. As money from international trade flooded into northern Italian cities and as the wealthy citizenry sought ways to spend their newfound wealth, painters stepped forward to express on their canvases and frescoes a newfound optimism for life. Unprecedented, energetic, and avant-garde for their time, Renaissance painters presented an abundance of different subjects and styles that attracted the attention of local patrons.

The sensational new art was quickly exported from Italy to other areas. Many northern Italian cities, led by Florence, became attractive for vacationers who flocked there to learn about new genres of art and to purchase paintings to take back with them to decorate their homes. Even the leaders of the Catholic Church entered the art market by sending messengers to commission major works from new young artists. Part of the attraction of visiting Florence became wandering the streets in search of the workshops where painters executed their works.

As the demand for paintings increased, cities such as Florence began to attract more young men eager to learn how to paint. Seeking to learn the new styles and forms of the early Renaissance, hundreds of young developing painters moved to Florence to apprentice themselves to one of several master painters. Once they found a master whose painting style and personality matched their own, they entered into a long-term apprenticeship that would teach them the fundamentals of Renaissance art.

IMITATING NATURE: "MISTRESS OF ALL MASTERS"

Imitating nature became the first objective—and the ultimate essence—of

Renaissance art. Painters committed years to the faithful reproduction of all that the eye could see. The more faithfully they depicted nature on their canvases and frescoes, the more perfect their work appeared. Many Renaissance painters articulated the importance of copying nature. The late-fourteenth-century painter and writer Cennino Cennini, for example, wrote in his book *The Craftsman's Handbook*, "Mind you, the most perfect steersman you can have, and the best helmsman, lie in the triumphal gateway of copying from nature. And this out does all models; and always rely

As the artistic center of Italy during the Renaissance, Florence's studios and streets bustled with people in search of beautiful works of art.

on this with a stout heart."[1] Fifty years later, Leon Battista Alberti echoed Cennini in his book *On Painting:* "Great is the force of anything drawn from nature. For this reason always take from nature that which you wish to paint, and always choose the most beautiful."[2]

Imitating nature became the guiding principle among Renaissance painters. The most viewed and analyzed painting ever executed, Leonardo da Vinci's *La Gioconda,* known today throughout the world as the Mona Lisa, achieved

Leonardo da Vinci's Mona Lisa became a model for Renaissance painters, who strove to imitate the painting's natural style.

its celebrated reputation because of its remarkable mirroring of Mona Lisa's face. Giorgio Vasari, an art historian who lived toward the end of the Renaissance in the mid–sixteenth century, praised the painting, as did many of his compatriots, because he understood its remarkable perfection as an imitation of nature:

Whoever desires to see how far art can imitate nature, may do so by observing this head [Mona Lisa] wherein every subtlety and every peculiarity have been faithfully reproduced. The eyes are bright and moist, and around them are those pale, red and slightly livid circles seen in life, while the lashes and eyebrows are represented with the closest exactitude with the separate hairs drawn as they issue from the skin, every turn being followed and all the pores exhibited in the most natural manner. The nose, with its beautiful and delicate red nostrils might easily be believed to be alive.[3]

Leonardo da Vinci himself paid tribute to the early-fifteenth-century painter Masaccio's ability to copy nature while insisting that other painters use nature as their standard. "Masaccio showed by his perfect works," said Leonardo, "how those who take for their standard anything but nature—mistress of all masters—weary themselves in vain."[4]

Realism applied to every aspect of painting, even depicting something so seemingly rudimentary as the darkness. To accurately accomplish this, painters experimented to perfect a technique called chiaroscuro, meaning "light and dark." This technique uses the intersection of light and dark in a painting to create forms that seem to disappear mystically into darkness. Complimenting Raphael on his perfect use of chiaroscuro Vasari once said, "As a work reproducing the effect of night this picture is truer than any other, and it is universally regarded as outstanding and inspired."[5]

Reputations were built on realism. Fra Filippo Lippi, for example, was commissioned to paint a biblical scene in the Strozzi Chapel in Florence in which Saint Philip calls forth a snake from a hole beneath a stone altar. When Lippi had completed the fresco, all agreed that he had executed it with extraordinary realism, but an incident that occurred shortly after elevated Lippi in the eyes of Florentine art patrons to the status of genius. According to the story, a young man was wandering in the Strozzi Chapel carrying a small stolen object. Hearing voices and fearing that he might be caught, the man looked for a hiding place for the object and spotted the painted hole. Mistakenly thinking it was real, he ran to hide his contraband in it, and as Vasari reported, "he ran in haste to this hole, but was foiled."[6]

Even though early Renaissance painters had greatly improved their ability to copy subjects such as people, trees, and buildings, an important ingredient was still missing. When copying real objects onto a canvas, even when copied accurately, some objects often looked out of proportion to others. To correct this type of distortion, early painters learned from the architect Filippo Brunelleschi about perspective.

PERSPECTIVE: MIRRORING NATURE ON A TWO-DIMENSIONAL SURFACE

Realism took another major step forward when the importance of perspective was discovered. Perspective is a mathematical system using geometry that describes how to represent three-dimensional objects found in nature on two-dimensional surfaces such as canvases and walls.

Perspective is based on the optical principle that objects close to a viewer appear larger and more detailed than distant objects. Art from the very early Renaissance that failed to depict perspective accurately appeared flat, poorly proportioned, and sometimes even comical when, for example, people standing next to a church were the same height as the church.

Once Florentine painters discovered the geometry of accurate perspective, they recognized its importance to realism and wanted to learn how to apply

꒦ GIORGIO VASARI ꒨

Giorgio Vasari is often credited as the father of art history. Born in 1511, his value to the understanding of Renaissance artists cannot be exaggerated. When he published his book *The Lives of the Artists,* first in 1550 and then again, in an expanded edition, in 1568, it was the first time that anyone dedicated an entire book to the biographies of the Renaissance masters. Vasari's biographies also allowed contemporary art enthusiasts to gain an appreciation of the history of the time and place.

Vasari did not personally know the early Renaissance masters because many predated him, so he was forced to rely heavily on whatever letters were available in private collections and on scattered references made by the painters' contemporaries. Working without volumes of documentation, Vasari often indulged in circulating stories, telling fanciful anecdotes that, although amusing, were frequently inaccurate.

Many of Vasari's chapters covering the early Renaissance artists are short. The biographies of men he knew during the closing years of the Renaissance, on the other hand, are considerably more complete and more detailed.

Vasari, a painter himself, counted as his friends the great triad of the late Renaissance: Leonardo da Vinci, Michelangelo, and Raphael. Fortunately for modern students of Renaissance art, the later biographies tell a more personal story than those of the artists Vasari did not know. The drawback, however, is that Vasari tended to be excessive in his praise for his friends; in fact, modern scholars often discount much of what he says because of his lack of objectivity. Nonetheless, Vasari is considered the most valuable primary source for information on Renaissance artists.

Renaissance writer, painter, and art historian Giorgio Vasari.

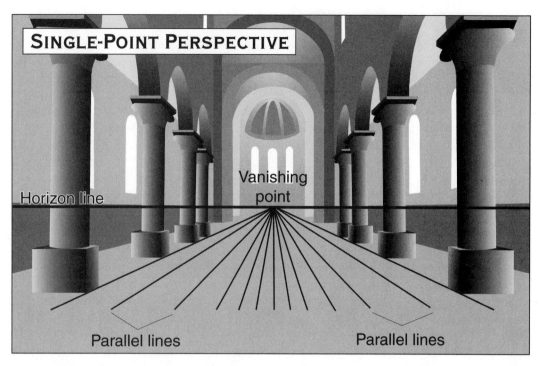

SINGLE-POINT PERSPECTIVE

Vanishing point

Horizon line

Parallel lines   Parallel lines

it. According to the painter and teacher Alberti, "Perspective geometry is among the first rudiments [basic principles] of the art of painting."[7] Albrecht Dürer, a German Renaissance painter who had heard about the perspective of Florentine painters, said, "I want to ride there to learn the secrets of the art of perspective."[8]

All of the great masters worked to perfect perspective. The celebrated Leonardo da Vinci, one of the great practitioners of perspective, told his apprentices that, of the many academic subjects necessary for painters to master, "The first is arithmetic and the second geometry . . . from these is born perspective, devoted to all the functions of the eye."[9]

Not all painters took Leonardo's recommendation seriously. One who did not was Titian and, because he had failed to master perspective, some believed his paintings were not worthy of being considered great masterpieces. Vasari told a story about Michelangelo seeing a newly completed painting by Titian called the *Nude Diana.* Everyone standing before the painting praised it, except for Michelangelo, who observed: "If this artist had been aided by art and knowledge of design [geometry], as he is by nature, he would have produced works which none could surpass, especially in imitating life."[10] Vasari then added to Michelangelo's observation, "It is quite true that without much study of drawing and of the

✒ THE MAGIC OF PERSPECTIVE ҩ

Painters during the Middle Ages were incapable of applying perspective to their paintings because they did not understand the mathematics involved. It was not until about 1400 that several Florentine artists, led by the brilliant architect Filippo Brunelleschi, defined the mathematics that accurately represent perspective. The Florentine painters Masaccio and Paolo Uccello were among the first to use Brunelleschi's rules to achieve the illusion of perspective in paintings. The use of perspective improved realism in painting so dramatically that many viewed its application as magical.

Perspective is based on elementary laws of optics, most notably the fact that distant objects appear smaller and less distinct than near objects. The most well-known example of this optical phenomenon is that of straight parallel railroad tracks that appear to converge and finally meet at a point in the distance. This point of conversion is called the vanishing point because all things seem to vanish the farther they are from the viewer. A scene in a painting may have more than one vanishing point depending on the alignment of the objects in the scene. For example, houses, buildings, and roads can all have vanishing points as they appear to recede into the background of a painting.

The perspective applied to a painting by an artist is also used to establish where the painter is standing relative to what is being painted. For example, a painter may choose to depict an aerial view of buildings by showing rooftops, a side view by painting a perspective that reveals only the sides of buildings, or a front-and-center perspective by painting only the fronts of buildings. It is important to note, however, that only one perspective can be used in a painting that seeks to realistically render a scene.

best works ancient and modern, one can never give complete grace to a work of art."[11]

INDIVIDUAL ARTISTIC STYLES

The development of individual artistic styles was the next natural progression among Renaissance painters. Just as early Renaissance masters had been valued and praised for perfecting the art of imitating nature, their successors were equally praised for developing unique artistic styles.

One of the first artists to recognize the importance of developing individual styles was Cennini, who made the observation that developing one's own style is critical for success:

If you follow the course of one master through constant practice, your intelligence would have to be crude indeed for you not to get some nourishment from him. Then you will find, if nature has granted you any imagination at all, you will eventually acquire a style individual to yourself and it cannot help being good. [12]

Certain Renaissance masters developed rich personal stylistic traits in their adventurous use of color, in their extravagant depiction of beautifully flowing hair and robes, and in their rendering of highly expressive faces depicting the emotions of joy, sadness, and fear. As the evolution of style progressed, art critics of the time used abstract terms to attempt to capture a painter's style. Masaccio's style, for example, was often described as being "pure and without ornateness," Botticelli's as being "manly," and Fra Angelico's as "ornate and pious."

The trend toward unique painting styles enabled art lovers to look at any work and immediately know the artist. In 1457, in a court dispute over a painting, an art connoisseur appeared as a witness to identify the artist of a particular

A comparison of two Renaissance paintings highlights their artists' distinct styles. Masaccio's Two Cripples *(left) illustrates his strong and simple style while Fra Angelico's* Paradise *is intricate and filled with busy detail.*

set of paintings. The witness was certain that the painter was Andrea Mantegna, because as he said, "Among painters, it is always known by whose hand any painting is, especially when it is by the hand of any established painter." [13]

The development of individual styles was very much appreciated by art patrons and was one of the reasons painters became popular with the wealthy. In 1505, the wealthy patron Isabella d'Esti sent a letter to Leonardo da Vinci entreating him to paint "a youthful Christ executed with that sweetness and soft ethereal charm which is the peculiar excellence of your art." [14]

ACHIEVING SOCIAL ACCEPTABILITY

Toward the end of the Renaissance, paintings had improved dramatically, and the growing congregation of art supporters recognized that something new and exciting was afoot. As this transition gradually took place over a span of several generations, painters eventually emerged as people capable of making important cultural observations and contributions to the city and citizens of Florence. The success and growing prestige of master artists, and what they accomplished to arrive at the pinnacle of Florentine society, was recognized by Giovanni Santi, who summarized in a poem their many artistic accomplishments:

One sees, that first of all he [a painter] has a grasp

Of great drawing, which is the true foundation

Of painting, then, second, in him comes

A glowing adornment of Invention.

And then his diligence, his lovely color,

With all its planes and varying distances . . .

Perspective, which brings on in its train

Arithmetic and geometry. [15]

One man who understood and enjoyed the rising status of painters was Leonardo da Vinci, who at the end of his life was invited to live with the king of France. Leonardo was acutely aware of the low status afforded painters before him when he commented, "Certainly if painters were capable of praising their works in writing, as poets have done, I do not believe that painting would have been given such a bad name." [16]

Leonardo was clearly angered by everyone, but especially writers. The following poetic tirade shows Leonardo's feelings about painting:

If you call painting mechanical because it is primarily manual, in that the hands depict what is found in the imagination, you writers draft with your hands what is found in your mind. With justified complaints painting laments that it has been excluded from the number of the liberal arts, since she is the true daughter of nature and acts though the noblest sense. There it was wrong, O writers, to have left her outside the number of the liberal arts, since she embraces not only the works of nature but also an infinite number that nature never created. [17]

When the end of the Renaissance was in sight, painters finally achieved their objective of being valued as highly as those engaged in other forms of intellectual pursuits. In Florence, some masters such as Leonardo and Michelangelo attained the status of cultural icons as patrons competed for their time and willingly paid extravagant prices to buy their paintings.

No longer mere craftsmen struggling to achieve aesthetic respect, painters finally emerged into the family of artists. Many of their names achieved a legendary status among the population, and they finally appeared on the invitation lists for galas given by not only high society but also cardinals, popes, princes, and kings.

CHAPTER 2

EDUCATION IN
A *BOTTEGA*

Renaissance painters were not born with genetic predispositions to paint superlative masterpieces; they needed to be trained. The Renaissance painter Alberti expressed this view in his book *On Painting:* "Nothing is at the same time both new born and perfect."[18] Although famed for its art, Florence offered no formal schooling for artists. The only formal instruction available was for those pursuing established professions in law, medicine, philosophy, theology, or mathematics.

Since there were no schools offering courses in painting, all aspiring painters, without exception, learned their signature skills under the watchful eye of a master painter in a workshop called a *bottega.* The length of training with a master varied depending on each young man's work ethic, natural talent, and character. Even the most talented, those ultimately rising to the caliber of Michelangelo or Giotto, trained for three years

before qualifying to paint independently. Less talented apprentices, who represented the vast majority, remained in a *bottega* for ten to fifteen years before striking out on their own, and some never did. As far as Cennini was concerned, thirteen years apprenticing was a necessary and reasonable tenure:

> To begin as a shop boy studying for one year, to get practice in drawing, . . . next to learn how to work at all branches which pertain to our profession . . . for the space of a good six years. Then to get experience in painting . . . for six more years. If you follow other systems, you need never hope that [the apprentices] will reach any high degree of perfection.[19]

Spending many years of apprenticing was not for everyone, however.

Some young artists drifted from *bottega* to *bottega,* never staying longer than a year. Others changed masters because of personality conflicts, some because of harsh treatment, and some, like Giotto and Michelangelo, because they had learned all that their master had to offer.

Passing on to a *garzone* all of a master painter's insights, techniques, and tricks of the trade that had been learned over many years was a daunting task. Equally daunting was the obligation on the part of the young aspiring artist to learn them. To learn the skill and craft of painters, the *garzone* had no options other than working alongside a master painter observing and copying his talents.

In 1400, the artist and writer Cennini explained that aspiring painters came to Florence because they "want to find a master; and they bind themselves to him with respect for authority, undergoing an apprenticeship in order to achieve perfection in all this."[20] For young men in their early teens, such an odyssey often meant leaving behind the

A typical scene in a Renaissance painter's studio was that of a young apprentice painstakingly following the instruction of his master.

comfort and security of their families in small rustic towns for the commotion and uncertainties of cosmopolitan Florence.

HEADING FOR FLORENCE

During the Renaissance, Florence dominated the artistic landscape more than any other city. Any young man anxious to pursue the life of a painter had as his goal to study under one of the many masters who made Florence their home. Florence, although not the only city immersed in the swirl of art, had more famous artists working in its *botteghe* than any other European city. The renowned Florentine painter Perugino claimed that his master teacher repeatedly told him that Florence was "the place above all others where men attain perfection in all the arts, but especially in painting."[21] The three reasons for this, he explained, were the large number of art critics in Florence; the artists' need to work quickly and perfectly to make enough money to live in such an expensive city; and, because so many talented painters lived there, "rivalry between men of talent is there most keen."[22] The late-fifteenth-century painter Luca Signorelli added to Perugino's logic by explaining that he moved from his native city Siena "to Florence to see the works of the living masters as well as those of the old masters."[23]

What motivated teenage boys to leave home in hopes for a painter's life in the first place was a complicated question. One man who knew a great deal about it was Cennini, who understood these young men. In his book

This fifteenth-century map of Florence was created at the height of the Renaissance when the city led all of Europe in the number of master artists, aspiring painters, and art critics there.

❧ AN ART GUIDE TO FLORENCE ❧

Italian cities engaged each other in many competitions, including which city deserved the title of leading art center. In reality, however, Florence had no serious rivals for modern art. The city's claim to its undisputed artistic supremacy was supported by the first art guidebook published anywhere, *A Souvenir of Many Statues and Paintings in the City of Florence,* in 1510, by Francesco Albertini. Albertini documented what most Florentines openly boasted: Florence had emerged over the previous century as the most art-savvy city in Europe.

The publication of Albertini's guidebook also signaled the important role that art played as a major civic and tourist attraction. Art and the presence of many famous artists drew thousands of tourists and art lovers to the city each year to view its unrivaled collection and to shop for something interesting to decorate their homes.

Albertini's guidebook took tourists on a trek through the city streets. He described the cathedrals and major architectural treasures and then the many sculptures and paintings found inside them.

The Craftsman's Handbook, Cennini cites many of their motivations for pursuing the life of a painter:

> It is not without the impulse of a lofty spirit that some are moved to enter this profession. . . . Their intellect will take delight in drawing, provided their nature attracts them to it of themselves, without any master's guidance, out of loftiness of spirit. There are those who pursue it, because of poverty and domestic need, for profit and enthusiasm, for the profession too; but above all these are to be extolled the ones who enter the profession through a sense of enthusiasm and exaltation. [24]

The most difficult step for a young man who wished to apprentice himself in Florence was often admitting to his parents that he had an interest in the arts. Most fathers recoiled at the notion of their sons becoming painters because artists did not enjoy civic respectability or the income of the reputable professions of the day such as clergymen, bankers, traders, and merchants.

Many young painters, even the most famous such as Michelangelo, fought bitterly with their fathers over the subject of going to Florence. Biographer Ascanio Condivi explained that Michelangelo's desire to paint caused him to be

> resented and quite often beaten unreasonably by his father and

his father's brothers who being impervious to the excellence and nobility of art, detested it and felt that its appearance in their family was a disgrace.[25]

Some boys quit arguing with their parents and gave up their dreams of achieving greatness in Florence. Instead, they grew old performing dreary monotonous work in local shops and farms. Others, with stronger yearnings and broader streaks of independence, ran away from home and found their way to the backstreet *botteghe* of Florence. A fortunate few had the good luck to stumble upon an opportunity to leave their villages for the more exciting city. The greatest of the early Renaissance painters, Giotto di Bondone, was given such an opportunity. Vasari tells the amazing story of how the great master painter Cimabue discovered Giotto's genius while the young boy was tending his father's sheep:

One day Cimabue, going on business from Florence to Vespignano, found Giotto, while his sheep were feeding, drawing a sheep from nature upon a smooth and solid rock with a pointed stone, having never learnt from any one but nature. Cimabue, marveling at him, stopped and asked him if he would go and be with him. And the boy answered that if his father were con-

tent he would gladly go. Then Cimabue asked Bondone for him, and he gave him up to him, and was content that he should take him to Florence.[26]

Few, however, experienced the good fortune of Giotto. For the others, Cennini recommended that they enter the profession of painting by surrounding themselves with "Enthusiasm, Reverence, Obedience, and Constancy. And begin to submit yourself to the direction of a master for instruction as early as you can; and do not leave the master until you have to."[27]

FINDING THE RIGHT MASTER

Young men hoping to apprentice themselves to a master had little difficulty locating the forty to fifty *botteghe* in Florence because most were clustered within two or three of the city's sixteen *granfaloni,* or districts. Each *granfalon* took pride in its painters' workshops, and because of the fame they brought to the city, most Florentines knew where the most renowned masters could be found.

For most young boys arriving in Florence, their fathers were in charge of finding a good master. Every father wanted assurances that his son, who would be living either at the home of the master or at the *bottega,* would be treated fairly, would be safe and well fed, and would be learning from one of the city's best masters. There was no "right" approach to making this decision, and many people offered their ideas. Cennini felt strongly that an apprentice ought to "Take care to select the best [master] and the one who has the greatest reputation."[28] In 1493, the Florentine monk Savonarola delivered a sermon in which he answered the question of how to choose a master, suggesting that there was a mystical transfer of the master's creative energy to the apprentice:

What does the pupil look for in a master? I'll tell you. The master draws from his mind an image which his hands trace on paper and it carries the imprint of his idea. The pupil studies the drawing and tries to imitate it. Little by little, he appropriates the style of his master.[29]

Most young men sought apprenticeships in one of the large *botteghe* because they offered more opportunities to learn a larger variety of talents than smaller workshops could. There were easily fifty large studios in Florence. Though the *botteghe* differed in specialization

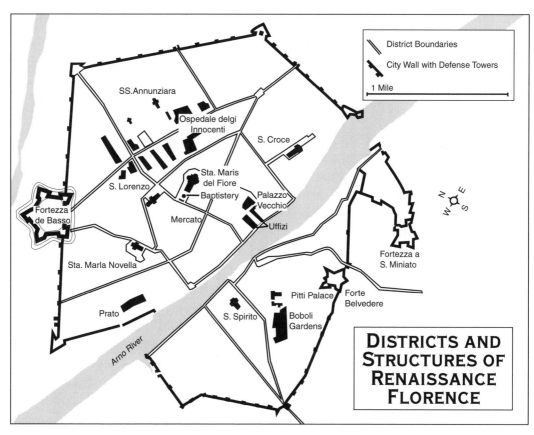

DISTRICTS AND
STRUCTURES OF
RENAISSANCE
FLORENCE

and quality of paintings, they basically performed the same function, providing artistic beauty to Florentines and thousands of visitors drawn to the city known for its art. An accomplished master who maintained one of the most famous *botteghe* in Florence was Domenico Ghirlandaio, who employed between fifty and sixty apprentices at any time. The most well-known master who employed no apprentices was Michelangelo, who, according to Vasari, avoided hiring them because "Michelangelo was a lover of solitude, devoted as he was to art. . . . It is true he was unfortunate in those [apprentices] whom he took into his shop. His apprentices were wholly unable to imitate their master." [30]

After a master was selected, a contract specifying conditions of work and pay was signed, for *garzoni* were not only studying with a master but working for him. Despite Michelangelo's father's anger at his son's insistence of choosing the life of an artist, like many good fathers, he accompanied his son to Florence, and selected Domenico Ghirlandaio as his son's master teacher. In 1488, the two men executed the following contract on behalf of the thirteen-year-old Michelangelo:

This 1st April that I Ludovico di Lionardo Buonarroti apprentice my son Michelangelo to Domenico [Ghirlandaio] and David di Tommaso di Currado for the next three years, with the following agreements: that the said Michelangelo shall remain, with them that time to learn to paint and practice that art and shall do what they bid him, and they shall give him 24 florins in the three years, 6 in the first, 8 in the second and 10 in the third. [31]

Not all contracts were so seemingly simple and good-natured. Conditions could be tough for apprentices, as is evidenced by a letter in which the master painter Neri di Bicci specified work conditions in his Florentine studio in 1456 for his seventeen-year-old apprentice Cosimo Rosselli:

Cosimo must come to my workshop at any time that suits me or I please, either day or night, and on holidays if necessary, to work diligently and work without taking any time off, and if he does take time off he must make it up. [32]

For many masters and their apprentices, a personal bond was established that lasted a lifetime. Whether the master was lenient or stern, many young boys were fortunate to find someone who recognized the paternal responsibilities of ensuring their well-being and safety. The master painter Raphael, for example, was known throughout Florence for his parental concerns. According to Vasari, Raphael "em-

Once established in a master's studio a young painter was responsible for studying his master's works.

ployed a large number of apprentices whom he assisted and instructed rather as a father than as artist to artist."[33] And Fra Bartolommeo, who was known to work his *garzoni* hard but compassionately, was affectionately nicknamed *il vetturale,* the mule driver, by his apprentices.

ACADEMICS IN THE *BOTTEGA*

Debate among master painters centered on the question of whether sub-jects other than painting should be taught in the *botteghe*. During the early Renaissance, Latin was no longer taught because Italian had become the common language in Italy and many Florentines questioned whether any other academic subjects were of value to aspiring painters. Master painters expressed conflicting views on this controversial topic.

Some masters such as the sculptor and painter Lorenzo Ghiberti believed

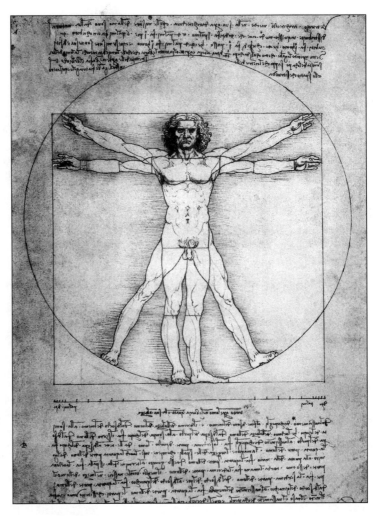

Leonardo da Vinci's Vitruvian Man, *a study in the proper proportion of the human body, shows the direct connection da Vinci made between art and geometry.*

that "Painters and sculptors should study grammar, geometry, arithmetic, astronomy, philosophy, history, medicine, anatomy, perspective, and theoretical design."[34] He could hardly have included many more disciplines on his list. Although the notion of the well-rounded thinker was popular during the Renaissance, other masters trimmed down Ghiberti's list. Alberti, for example, recommended

that painters learn all the liberal arts, but most of all they had to understand geometry. Leonardo da Vinci voiced his view that "A youth should first learn perspective and then the proportions of things."[35]

Mathematics, however, was not high on everyone's list of prerequisites for the successful painter. Cennini advised that the manner in which a new apprentice conducted his personal everyday life was far more important than what academic subjects he learned:

> Your life should always be arranged just as if you were studying theology, or philosophy, or other theories, that is to say, eating and drinking moderately, at least twice a day, electing digestible and wholesome dishes, and light wines. There is another cause which, if you indulge it, can make your hand so unsteady that it will waver more, and flutter far more, than leaves do in the wind, and this is indulging too much in the company of woman.[36]

In the end, studying geometry won out in most *botteghe*. It became indispensable, as Leonardo pointed out, for a proper understanding and execution of perspective in two-dimensional paintings and drawings. One painting master, Francesco Squarcione, signed a contract with each apprentice agreeing to teach

> The principle of a plane [flat surface] with lines drawn according to my method, and to put figures on the said plane . . . and teach him the system of a naked body, measured in front and behind, and to put eyes, nose, mouth, and ears in a man's head at the right measured places . . . to correct models for him, and correct his mistakes, as far as I can.[37]

Vasari took his own path on this topic, weighing in on the side of inspiration: "It is better far to live a balanced life than to give way to too severe studies. It is only when the spirit of inspiration is roused that good work is done; then only do great thoughts come, and only then are great things accomplished."[38]

LEARNING FROM THE MASTERS

Drawing copies of existing masterpieces was standard practice for all apprentices. Cennini gave advice to young painters to "take pains and pleasure in constantly copying the best things which [you] can find done by the hands of the great masters."[39] The Florentine teacher Gasparino Barzizza echoed Cennini's advice after observing several *botteghe* in Florence, noting that "Whenever something is to be learned from the master, they [the masters] are in the habit of handing them [the apprentices] some very good figures and pictures, as models of this craft, and taught by these, they can progress a bit by themselves."[40]

Not all practice occurred inside the *bottega*. Apprentices were encouraged to roam the streets of Florence in search of architectural motifs worthy of drawing, and in this regard, apprentices had a wealth of choices. Following the times of Giotto and the architect Brunelleschi, young sketchers spent hundreds of hours drawing some of the world's most famous architectural treasures found in Florence. Highest on the list were the dome of the church Santa Maria del Fiore, designed by Brunelleschi; the 270-foot-tall Campanile, also known as Giotto's Bell Tower; and the remarkable pair of sculpted bronze doors called the Gates of Paradise, executed by Ghiberti.

Young apprentices wandering the streets and piazzas sometimes found young ladies eating their lunches or reading on grassy knolls along the river. Such an opportunity to sketch was not overlooked, and many young artists used these unknowing models to perfect their technique for drawing long graceful tresses and subtle yet complex folds of dresses and capes. The accurate rendering of a dress was considered the mark of a master artist because the numerous hairpin turns of the fabric lying on top of one another

☙ LEARNING THE TRICKS OF THE TRADE ❧

Painters employed tricks of the trade just as other professions did. To achieve realistic-looking clothing on people, for example, the artist Filarete recommended soaking linen in glue and then draping it on a wooden figure. After the linen had hardened, sketchers and painters could take as much time as they wished to complete a fine rendering. Creighton Gilbert, in his book *Italian Art, 1400–1500,* includes a quotation by Filarete explaining why he preferred draping wood models to humans: "If you want to arrange it [the linen] another way, put it in hot water, and you can change it to another form, and draw from this figure what you want." The popularity of models made of wood, wax, marble, and clay is attested to by the sixty-three heads, hands, feet, and torsos used by apprentices in the *bottega* of the master painter Fra Bartolommeo.

Part of the painter's job was to experiment to find new painting techniques. Early Renaissance painters sought to develop a technique that would create a misty effect in the backgrounds of their paintings. Giotto was the first to discover that an illusion of mist rising from a meadow could be achieved by applying multiple layering of oils. He named the new trick *sfumato,* meaning "smoke."

Painters often struggled with the issue of balance in a painting. They wanted to fill the painting in such a way that all areas contained interesting objects yet, at the same time, focus the viewers' attention on the central subjects. Leonardo da Vinci was the first master to achieve both objectives; it took his rivals several years to understand and then copy. His solution was to geometrically arrange his most important subjects to form a triangle.

A fifteenth-century sketch, by an unknown artist, features a young painter as he sketches one of the many famous statues found in Renaissance Italy.

demanded attention to subtle transitions of shade and light.

The delicate rendering of facial expressions was equally demanding. All masters required perfection in the subtle highlighting where the sun bounced off the forehead, eyebrows, nose ridge, and cheekbones, and shadowing where dips shrouded the eyes, lips, jawline, and neck. Vasari relates the inclination of Leonardo da Vinci, who loved to follow people with unusual faces, sometimes for an entire day, "until he could draw them as well by memory as though they stood before him." [41]

STUDYING THE LIVING

Of all studies, that of the human body played the most significant role during the Renaissance. No subject was more difficult to render accurately, yet none was more often depicted. All Renaissance artists revered the careful and proportionally accurate rendering of the body done by Greek and Roman sculptors.

Learning to draw or paint a person was far more difficult than sketching Brunelleschi's dome or Giotto's Bell Tower. The body, even when standing motionless, twists and curves at the

❧ EGGS AND THE ARTIST ❧

Without eggs, Renaissance art might have been disappointing. Renaissance artists manufactured paints by mixing finely ground pigment, water, vinegar, and egg yolk. Eggs were used as the binding agent that held the ingredients of the paint together. When egg white is added to the medium, the paint dries more rapidly, and when applied by brush, it leaves minute brush-stroke lines that create an effect of the paint being dragged out on the wall.

Apprentices were ordered to perform the tedious work of grinding pigments into the egg yolk. The combination of egg yolk and powdered pigment created paint capable of lasting many centuries, if not a millennium—very early works are already six hundred years old.

The distinctive quality of egg-based tempera paint was that it allowed the paint to express any of three distinct properties depending on the look the painter wished to achieve. Tempera can be used as an opaque color, which permits a thick application of several layers of a single tone. It can also be used as an opalescence, which produces a rainbow effect of lighter tones applied over darker tones, or as a transparency, produced by painting darker tones over lighter ones.

legs, hips, shoulders, neck, and head. As one feature shifts, so do all the others to maintain balance. Masters sometimes paid live models to pose in their *botteghe* for apprentices; others expected the youngest and least experienced apprentices to pose for the older ones. According to Renaissance art historian Martin Wackernagel,

It was probably a duty of young apprentices as well as older assistants that they occasionally should be at their master's disposal as nude models, wholly unclothed or in light undergarments. Jacopo Sansovino, for example, had his *garzone,* Pippo del Fabro stand the whole day as a model. [42]

Frustration, however, quickly set in because the models were unable to hold a pose for more than fifteen to twenty minutes—not nearly long enough for sketchers to finish their drawings. To address the legitimate complaints of the models, they were given props to reduce muscle strain. Thus, some early drawings of figures depict the models resting their feet on boxes, leaning against a wood support, or occasionally grasping ropes to hold a position.

Not all painters, however, were willing to work with contrived props. Leonardo da Vinci refused to allow such nonsense; he insisted on actually seeing what he would paint. To accomplish such a setting yet keep his models, such as Mona Lisa, comfortable and alert, he paid musicians to play for them and jesters to amuse them. In the case of Mona Lisa, Vasari explains that the entertainment was successful in keeping

Wanting to paint what he actually saw, Leonardo da Vinci paid musicians and entertainers to coax a smile from the subject of his most renowned painting, Mona Lisa.

her from that look of melancholy so common in portraits. This painting, on the contrary, has so pleasing an expression and a smile so sweet that one must think of it divine rather than human. [43]

As an alternative to live models to achieve a detailed rendering of the human body, some painters and sketchers brought clay models or marble statues into the *botteghe*. Alberti recommended the use of clay and marble to study and copy the play of light and shadows across the surfaces. And Cennini made the correct observation that studying statues allowed the apprentice sketcher

> to notice where darks and half tones and highlights come; and this means you have to apply your shadows and washes of ink; to leave the natural grounds in the half tones; and to apply the highlights with white lead. [44]

Fra Bartolommeo devised yet another alternative to live models. He preferred to have real objects before him as he worked. To draw draperies, arms, and other things, he had a large wooden life-size model with movable joints, which he dressed in natural clothes. In this way, he was able to keep the figure in any position he desired until he had completed his sketch.

STUDYING THE DEAD

Painters understood that anatomically accurate renderings of the body required an understanding of what was hidden below the skin as well as what could be seen on the surface. To accomplish accurate rendering of muscle definition, skin texture, veins, and bone structure, some masters brought human corpses into their *botteghe* to be cut open and sketched. The theft of bodies from cemeteries occurred from time to time, regardless of laws against such clandestine activities. Grave robbers managed to scratch out a meager living supplying fresh corpses to the studios.

According to Condivi, Michelangelo perfected the rendering of the human body in part because his master had "provided him both with a room and with corpses for the study of anatomy, . . . nothing could give him greater pleasure." [45] If master painters were squeamish about buying illegal corpses, and many were, they could purchase dead relatives from poor families. The attraction to the poor of such macabre sales was money. Not only could they make more money from selling a dead relative than they could sweeping streets, but they were spared the cost of having a funeral. Dead bodies decayed quickly without refrigeration, and Condivi disclosed that Michelangelo once commented that he gave up dissecting corpses because "His long handling of them had so affected his stom-

A 1520 drawing depicts Renaissance artists, including Michelangelo (foreground with sketchpad), examining a cadaver in an anatomy lesson.

ach that he could no longer eat or drink healthfully."[46]

Interspersed with their artistic and academic studies, all *garzoni* were required to work in their masters' *botteghe* actually contributing to the creation of paintings. Such shifting of gears between the two distinctly different activities was the nature of an apprentice's life as a condition of his employment and as the best way to learn his art.

CHAPTER 3

WORKING IN
A *BOTTEGA*

The *bottega* was a place of hard work and frenetic energy from dawn till dusk. With the exception of Sundays and occasional holidays, each day was filled with dozens of tasks that were coordinated to focus the collective energy of the master and his apprentices on completing the commissions of clients. Such works, especially large ones, compelled everyone to work closely and in concert. Every worker, from the master down the line to the youngest apprentice, had specific assignments that were geared to produce the finest quality paintings possible. Each master took pride in his finished works, and each commonly spent as much of his time managing the everyday responsibilities of the workshop as he did painting.

The *bottega* provided a range of experiences and opportunities from which the apprentices derived their earliest understandings of painting.

All new *garzoni* quickly realized that there was far more to painting great works of art than brushing paint on a wood panel, stucco wall, or stretched canvas. Most also immediately realized that they would not have an opportunity to actually paint for their first four or five years. They would have to learn the hard work of preparing to paint before trying their hands at the more leisurely and prestigious application of paint.

THE WORKDAY

Dawn signaled the start of the workday as young *garzoni* ran down the streets of Florence to get to their *botteghe* on time. The Via Tosconella was one of the more celebrated Florentine streets; the sounds and commotion of several art studios there acted as beacons to attract art shoppers. Another famous street was the Via Ghibellina, a favored destination for tourists, where Michelangelo worked. Like many other streets in Florence, these were narrow, twisting cobblestone streets lined with four-story stone and brick buildings. The *botteghe* were always housed on the ground floor of the buildings, making it easy for anyone to wander in off the street to observe the day's activities, gain an idea of the type and quality of paintings being produced, and hopefully make a purchase.

Domenico Ghirlandaio had one of the most well-known *botteghe* in Florence. Housed in a large building, Ghirlandaio's workshop was arranged around an internal courtyard hidden from the street. The main entry opened onto the street, flanked by one or two low walls that could be used as benches or counters for displaying merchandise. Small windows along the street permitted limited light inside, which dictated

A sketch of fifteenth-century Florence shows a maze of narrow streets and dense blocks of ground-floor apartments, which housed the city's master artists and their studios.

the workday from midmorning to late afternoon. On warm days, however, the large central courtyard was a favorite place to work; it provided better light than what could be found inside and extended the workday by several hours.

The activity of the shops tended to spill out beyond the overhangs and walls into the street. Here, apprentices leaned completed portraits—along with priming materials, varnishes, and glued wood frames—against the workshop walls to dry in the sun. This grand display of paintings and drying materials also served to advertise the fine artistic qualities of Ghirlandaio's craft to tourists wandering the streets in search of mementos to take home. Fascinated by the quantity and quality of what they saw, many took the time to enter the studio for a closer look.

Renaissance artists displayed small collections of art, like the one pictured, just outside their workshops to entice strolling tourists and wealthy patrons inside for a closer look.

✂ THE ART OF MAKING PAINTBRUSHES ✂

Renaissance painters made their own paint-brushes from two types of hairs: those from the tails of ermine called minever brushes, and those from hog skins called bristle brushes. Each had different uses, because the ermine hairs were much finer and softer than the hairs of hogs. Cennini described the manufacture of the bristle brush in his book The Craftsman's Handbook.

The bristle brushes are made in this style. First get bristles of a white hog, for they are better than black ones; but see that they come from a domestic hog. And make up with them a large brush into which go a pound of these bristles; and tie it to a good-sized stick with a plowshare bight or knot. And this brush should be limbered up by whitewashing walls, and wetting down walls where you are going to plaster; and limber it up until these bristles become very supple. Then undo this brush, and make the divisions of it as you want, to make a brush of any variety. And make some into those which have the tips of all the bristles quite even—those are called "Blunt" brushes; and some into pointed ones of every sort of size. Then make little sticks of the wood mentioned above, and tie up each little bundle with double waxed thread. Put the tip of the little stick into it, and proceed to bind down evenly half the length of this little bundle of bristles, and farther up along the stick; and deal with them all in the same way.

Once inside the large interior room and its many side rooms, visitors experienced the sights, sounds, and smells of the daily activities needed to create art. The sounds of saws cutting wood that would later be carved into beautiful picture frames painted with gold echoed throughout the studio. The sounds of hammers pounding iron nails to join wood panels made conversation nearly impossible. The smells of the paint room—the fragrances of finely ground minerals and flowers mixed into the paints to create delicate hues—filled the air.

One entire room was dedicated to the task of preparing canvases for Ghirlandaio. The apprentices stretched the canvas on a wood frame and then covered it with many layers of a primer called gesso made of glue, egg white, and a plaster substance containing crushed chicken bones. In another room, paintbrushes of varying shapes and sizes, made from stiff pig hairs, could be seen being made. The brushes had to meet several needs. Some were used in the painting of small portraits the size of a person's palm, while others were used to compose large frescoes covering the ceilings and walls of churches.

SWEATY WORK

Hidden from the inquisitive eyes of customers, first-year apprentices learned the sweaty side of the painter's life. Although the conditions and experiences of apprenticeship varied among the scores of *botteghe* in Florence, this system of training remained firmly entrenched as a standard for the duration of the Renaissance.

First-year apprentices, often in their early teens and occasionally younger, could expect to start at the bottom of the pecking order. In a small shop with two or three boys, or a large one with as many as fifty, the newest apprentice could expect to be handed the most menial tasks. Such drudgery included sweeping the floors of the shop when all others had left for the day; running the streets in search of needed art supplies; erecting scaffolding at work locations away from the *bottega;* unloading heavy materials such as wood, marble, and iron clamps; and even cooking meals. In exchange for such servile duties, the newcomer had the opportunity to observe the master and his staff at work.

Over time, additional jobs relating to art would be handed to the apprentices. They would perform basic sketching, prepare wood panels for painting, apply stucco to walls for frescoes, learn the art of making different types of paintbrushes, and, most important, learn the skill of making paint. By carrying out such an impressive array of tasks, *garzoni* were able to advance their own artistic development.

GRINDING PAINT

Paints could not be bought in Renaissance Florence. Each master appointed young apprentices to learn the craft of making paints because large quantities were frequently needed and because painters prided themselves in their ability to create new colors that were not found anywhere else in Florence. Patrons, like their painters, delighted in showing off colors that their friends had never seen.

Grinding and mixing paint was an important yet tedious task. Few masters would even consider performing the hours of monotonous grinding, and even assistants passed it off to the youngest new apprentice. To emphasize the tediousness of the grinding process, Condivi commented that Michelangelo "finished the work [on one of his frescoes] in twenty months, without any help whatever, not even someone to grind his colors for him."[47]

Before the grinding could start, the pigment had to be found. Gathering pigments was an enjoyable task for the apprentice because it meant being free to run around the city far from the watchful eye of the master. The colors came mainly from minerals such as cobalt, azurite, and lapis lazuli for blues; malachite and verdigris for greens; alkaline chromate for orange; and porphyry and hematite for reds. All of these minerals could be bought at a pharmacy because they were also used in a variety of medicines.

Vegetation was the second most plentiful source of pigments. Among the vegetable extracts used were various berries, roots, flower petals, and vines. Spices such as saffron to create yellow, red pepper seed for burnt-red,

and almond shells and peach stones for various shades of black were also used. To acquire these vegetable sources, young *garzoni* scurried down the streets to the *Mercato Vecchio* (Old Marketplace), where everything edible was available for sale.

When an unusual color was needed that could not be found in Florence, apprentices were sent out to the country to find it. Cennini remembered as

A sketch dated 1503 shows an apprentice painter grinding paint.

an apprentice being sent into the hills in search of a particular yellow:

> Upon reaching a little valley, a very wild steep place, scraping the steep with a spade, I beheld seams of many kinds of color: ocher, dark and light, blue, and white, . . . and this I held the greatest wonder in the world—that white could exist in a seam in the earth. [48]

Cennini was so particular about his yellow hues that he identified six distinct yellow tones from different mineral soils.

On rare occasions, apprentices went to the meadows to collect insects and, on even rarer occasions, to the seashore to grub for mollusks and shells as sources of pigments. Sea urchins, for example, produced a dazzling indigo and certain shells produced deep blacks and iridescent silver.

Once the apprentice arrived at the *bottega* with the pigments, the real work of grinding began. The initial grinding took place in a mortar, but because the finest powder possible made the most brilliant color, a second grinding was done on a marble

✺ CREATING BLACK PAINT ✺

To the trained eye, no two black paints were the same. Painters often used several different shades of black and, therefore, needed to know several techniques for making the color. Cennini, in his book The Craftsman's Handbook, *discusses several interesting methods for creating different shades of black.*

Know that there are several kinds of black colors. There is black which is made from vine twigs; these twigs are to be burned; and when they are burnt, throw water on them, and quench them; and then work them up like the other black. And this is a color both black and lean and it is one of the perfect colors we employ. There is another black which is made from burnt almond shells or peach stones, and this is a perfect black. There is another black which is made in this manner; take a lamp full of linseed oil, and fill the lamp with this oil, and light the lamp. Then put it so lighted, underneath a good clean baking dish, and have the little flame of the lamp come to the bottom of the dish, two or three fingers away, and the smoke which comes out of the flame will strike on the bottom of the dish, and condense in a mass. Wait a while; take the baking dish, and with some implement sweep the color, that is, this soot, off on to a paper, or in some dish; and it does not need to be worked up or ground, for it is a very fine color.

slab with a stone rolling pin to further pulverize the pigment material. After hours of this laborious work, the pigment was then ground on a sheet of glass until the master was satisfied that the pigment had reached as fine a dust as was reasonable. Masters and their *garzoni* had more arguments over the issue of how long to grind a pigment than any other. The reason for tension was evident when reading the master painter Cennini's instruction to one complaining *garzone:* "When you have got it powdered, put some clear water on it, and work it up as much as you can; for if you were to work it for ten years, it would constantly become more perfect." [49]

YOUTHFUL EXUBERANCE IN THE WORKSHOP

Although the work of an apprentice inside the *botteghe* could be tedious and stressful, it could also have its fun moments for creative young minds, especially when the master left the workshop. Vasari tells the following story about Giotto to illustrate the exuberance that could occur in the workshops:

It is said that while Giotto was still a boy, and with [his master] Cimabue, he once painted a fly on the nose of a figure which Cimabue had made. The fly was so natural that, when his master turned round to go on with his

work, he more than once attempted to chase the fly away with his hand, believing it to be real, before he became aware of his mistake. [50]

Giotto was not the only precocious painter to develop a reputation for enjoying practical jokes in the *botteghe* at the expense of the masters. According to Condivi, the young apprentice Michelangelo had been given a drawing of a head to copy, and he

rendered it so precisely that when he returned the copy in place of the original [, at] first the owner did not detect the deception, but discovered it only when the boy was telling a friend of his and laughing about it. Many wanted to compare the two, and they found no difference because, apart from the perfection of the copy, Michelangelo had used smoke to make it seem as old as the original. This gained him a considerable reputation. [51]

Youthful exuberance, however, sometimes led to unanticipated trouble. The young apprentice Pietro Torrigiano, who had a reputation for being a troublemaker, earned his only claim to fame while a group of Ghirlandaio's apprentices was sketching an altar painted by Masaccio. When Torrigiano compared his sketch with that of Michelangelo's,

This self-portrait of Michelangelo dated 1540 reveals his crooked nose, broken in a youthful fistfight with another artist.

the two began a heated argument over the merits of their sketches that escalated to personal insults and then a fistfight at the altar. The fight ended when Torrigiano landed a punch square on Michelangelo's nose, breaking it and splattering blood over the altar. The nose never properly healed, and later in life, Michelangelo's self-portraits always depicted his crooked broken nose.

THE MASTER AND HIS SENIOR *GARZONI*

The actual work of painting was the domain of the master and his older apprentices. The master of a *bottega,* besides being the master painter, shouldered responsibilities as the owner, teacher, production manager, accountant, arbitrator of all disputes, and surrogate father. He could not do everything alone and relied heavily on his senior *garzoni* for help.

The older apprentices rose through the ranks in a *bottega* by acquiring the skills needed to execute high-quality preliminary sketches for frescoes, called cartoons, and actual paintings. Each apprentice had the same objective: to learn the skills, techniques, and secrets of his master that would be the pass-port to opening his own *bottega*. But until that time, the apprentices played a pivotal role in the smooth functioning of their masters' shops.

The older seasoned assistants worked closely with the master on the more sophisticated tasks of designing, drawing cartoons, and applying paint.

☙ THE *BOTTEGA* AS SALESROOM ❧

The *bottega* was frequently the best setting for viewing an artist's work and for negotiating commissions. A busy workshop was a good sign to potential clients that the master's works were sought after by many art patrons. Master painters with large studios and many apprentices could display an impressive array of different types of works in various states of completion to potential customers.

Visits from vacationers and art patrons from foreign countries were commonplace in Florence. One of the favorite pastimes of many tourists was to designate a day or two to walk the streets in search of charming studios. Of interest to vacationers were the studios of the old masters as well as the young up-and-coming masters whose works could be bought for considerably less money than those of established painters.

Well-dressed visitors who wandered into a studio were greeted by a knowledgeable senior apprentice charged with the responsibility of escorting them around the studio, answering questions, suggesting available works that they might appreciate, and above all else, making a sale. Tourists enjoyed returning home with a small wood panel painting to hang in their homes while boasting to family and friends about the fame of the artist as one of the best in Florence—whether it was true or not.

Visits to the *botteghe* by wealthy art patrons were another matter. Such visits were rare, so when they occurred, there was great significance attached to them. When a recognized Florentine art patron entered a studio unannounced, a frenzy of activity followed. No art patron in Florence carried greater importance to painters than Lorenzo de Medici, the most powerful and one of the wealthiest men in Florence. In 1494, Lorenzo visited the studio of Andrea Mantegna, where Lorenzo "saw with great pleasure various paintings by the said Andrea, and certain sculptured heads and many other antique pieces, by which it seems he was much delighted."

Occasionally they were given the opportunity to take charge of small commissions for tourists. In such cases, the master often handed the entire job to a senior assistant. In so doing, both benefited; while the master made money on the project, the assistant honed his skills and moved closer to gaining his independence.

Most assistants were involved with frescoes. A master painter such as Ghirlandaio executed the design and the more demanding painting such as figure outlines, faces, and any details requiring expert technique. The rest was turned over to apprentices, under the supervision of the master, as learning experiences. Huddling high above a cathedral floor, the team of assistants worked side by side painting objects secondary to the main theme such as clothing, furniture, background scenery, and architectural features.

Some masters were reluctant to allow assistants to become overly involved in the execution of a painting or fresco. One reason for this was that most masters derived great satisfaction in seeing the completion of their own labor and in the accompanying adulation. A second very different reason was that master painters were worried

When a wealthy patron pays a visit to a Renaissance painter's studio, attention in the studio quickly shifts from the production of art to the needs of the paying client.

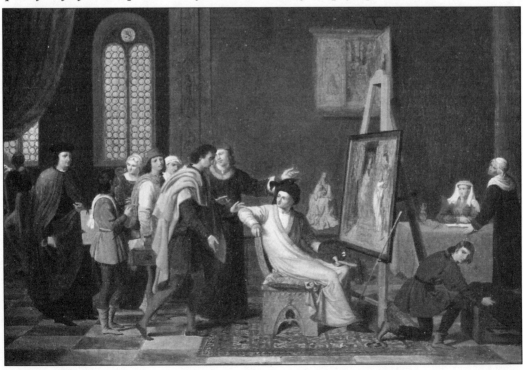

that they might become known as a painter whose artistic treasures were actually completed by the hands of *garzoni*.

Yet, for those such as Bernardino Pinturicchio, who acquired a reputation for using a great number of assistants, the financial rewards could be satisfying. As Vasari observed, however, relying too heavily on assistants could lower the quality of the painting: "Pinturicchio gave satisfaction to princes and nobles because his staff worked fast. . . . Such works may be, however, less excellent than those of masters who proceed more slowly on their own and with greater deliberation."[52]

A few rare apprentices possessed such extraordinary artistic skills that they were admired beyond their fellow assistants and even beyond their masters. One such assistant was Michelangelo, who was under contract to work in the *bottega* of Ghirlandaio. Michelangelo's genius was discovered by his master one day when he left a fresco he was painting to go to lunch. According to Vasari, while Ghirlandaio was gone,

> Michelangelo drew the scaffolding, trestles, pots of paint, brushes, and the apprentices at their tasks. When he returned, Domenico Ghirlandaio was amazed at the power and originality of the lad's work. "This boy knows more than I do!" he exclaimed.[53]

The workshops of Florence proved to be fruitful environments for preparing aspiring artists, yet they had limitations. Most were too small to train apprentices in the skills needed to execute large canvases and none could possibly instruct them in the skills required to execute frescoes. In order to advance to the higher level of large commissions, masters took their *garzoni* to sites outside the *botteghe*.

CHAPTER 4

WORKING OUTSIDE A *BOTTEGA*

Not every artistic commission could be carefully crafted within the comfort and convenience of a *bottega*. Many of the major works commissioned by the church or patrician families were site specific, created for particular locations that required specific calculations and unique preparations. Such works were often far too large or too complicated to be produced in a studio for later on-site installation. So, much of the work had to be performed where the final product would be installed, which was often many days from Florence on horseback. In addition to the complications of distant locations, such commissions also frequently involved personal sacrifice, engineering problems, dangers, and deprivations not encountered in the relative comfort of the *bottega*.

TRAVEL WITH FAMILIES

Many of the most sought-after fresco painters lived nomadic lives, moving from city to city. Living away from home was a test of will for a single painter, and even more difficult for a painter with a family. Renaissance writers were sometimes quick to point out that very few of the great painters ever married. Michelangelo, Raphael, Alberti, Masaccio, Botticelli, Verrocchio, Leonardo da Vinci, and Piero di Cosimo, among others, remained single throughout their lives.

When an artist was married and had a family, however, the difficulties of painting away from home were compounded. For a family man such as Giotto, who had established a reputation for himself in Florence, leaving home for two years to paint a fresco was an expensive and daunting endeavor. Although relatively little is known about Giotto's family, it appears that the family remained close together, often traveling with him from commission to commission.

When Giotto was invited by the Scrovegni family in Padua to paint the interior of the Arena Chapel, he took his entire family (his wife and eight children) with him. Because the city was far from Florence, about one hundred miles, Giotto could not afford to pay the transportation and living expenses of his *garzoni.* To solve the problem of being without his apprentices, Giotto established an art studio in the relatively remote city to train local boys and put all of his children to work on the huge fresco.

Giotto was one of the few fresco painters to solve his apprentice problem by employing his own children and by establishing a school to train local talented adolescents. In this regard, Giotto was one of the most industrious and innovative painters of the early Renaissance. When the fresco was finished in 1305, he departed Padua with his family but left the school intact for the future benefit of the city.

PAINTING FRESCOES: THE HIGHEST CALLING

"In the name of the Most Holy Trinity I wish to start you on painting." [54] With this powerful invocation indicating the

Padua, depicted here in this 1540 sketch, was one of many key Italian cities that commissioned artworks from painters based in Florence.

seminal significance of fresco painting, Cennini began his chapter titled "The Method and System for Painting on a Wall, that is, in Fresco." Cennini was not the only master who believed that painting a fresco was the highest calling for a painter. Most painters agreed with him because, unlike canvas and wood paintings, frescoes painted on walls and ceilings were of immense sizes, they exhibited a more varied palate of brilliant colors, and they provided the space for more powerful and interesting subjects. Unfortunately for painters, the fresco was the one painting that could not be executed in the *bottega.*

A fresco commission meant summoning all human resources available in a *bottega.* No other form of painting demanded as much time-consuming planning, preparation, and execution. A commission to paint a fresco covering several thousand square feet of plaster was a lengthy undertaking that might keep some workers away from home for a year or two and sometimes longer (Michelangelo, for example, committed four years to the ceiling of the Sistine Chapel).

The first step in the design process justified the years of studying mathematics and geometry as a *garzone.* Crucial to a perfectly executed fresco was a perfectly measured wall laying out the dimensions to be decorated. Precise calculations began with determining the area to be painted, locating dead-center points along both the vertical and horizontal lines of symmetry, and determining if the surface was perfectly vertical and if all walls joined the ceiling and floor at right angles. A final mathematical description of the surface provided a geometric road map for positioning and properly balancing all the figures on the fresco.

The first step in the actual painting was the outlining of all major figures. This crucial task was usually reserved for the master who had drawn most, if not all, of the cartoons on paper that would be transferred to the plaster. Some masters outlined all figures freehand with charcoal; others held each individual paper cartoon in place and tapped charcoal through small perforations along the outlines to leave a charcoal outline on the plaster when the apprentices removed the cartoons. When the entire fresco had been outlined with charcoal, the master reviewed the totality from the floor to ensure proper spacing, proportions, and definition. If changes were required, now was the time to make them.

When the master declared the outline ready, the temporary charcoal lines were painted over with permanent red ocher. The secret to a long-lasting fresco is the application of wet paint on fresh wet stucco in a process called *buon fresco,* meaning "true fresco." It is the moisture in the paint that bleeds into the moisture of the stucco that permanently bonds the paint to the wall.

❧ THE GEOMETRY OF A FRESCO ☙

Early Renaissance painters made long strides toward developing the geometry necessary for the perfect representations of three-dimensional objects on the two-dimensional plane of a wall. Correctly and accurately measuring and marking the walls before the application of paint was essential to ensure proper proportions and spacing.

Leonardo was one of the principal proponents of geometry in all of his works. With regard to his use of perspective, which required an understanding of geometry, Leonardo successfully employed it to create his masterpiece, the *Last Supper,* painting on a wall of Santa Maria delle Grazie in Milan, Italy. Leonardo faced the problem that the wall was unusually long and narrow, fifteen by thirty feet. To achieve the proper perspective was a tricky proposition for the master.

There have been recent discoveries of how Leonardo applied geometry to achieve the fresco's perspective. A hole in the wall has been recently discovered into which a nail had been driven, located near the forehead of Jesus. The location is the key spatial focus of Leonardo's painting. He drove a nail into the wall and radiated string in various directions to help him see the perspective of the room he was painting.

The strings used by Leonardo were coated with chalk and after he measured the lengths, he snapped the lines, leaving behind the chalk impressions. In addition to the use of lines, Leonardo as well as other fresco painters, used a plumb bob (a brass weight hanging from a string that creates a perfectly vertical line) for lines running from top to bottom. In addition to strings and plumb bobs, compasses were another mathematical tool used to find and mark precise angles for lines radiating across a wall.

Leonardo da Vinci created the Last Supper *using geometry.*

Since the final application of plaster covers the painted outline, the master painter and his apprentices applied the final wet coat only to small sections at a time while referencing the paper cartoon. This process of covering the outlines with wet stucco was clarified by Berkeley resident and Renaissance scholar and portrait artist Michael Fuller, who explained in an interview, "Areas requiring little detail, such as distant landscape scenes, could be completed in large sections in a matter of hours, whereas areas requiring great detail, such as a person's face, might be done in several small sections over a period of a day or two."[55]

DANGEROUS WORKING CONDITIONS

Painting a fresco in a city far from the comforts and conveniences of art-smart Florence had its liabilities. The most difficult and dangerous problems of some frescoes involved working high in the air. Scaffolding was erected to support painters and their assistants while painting ceilings, walls, and altars far above cathedral floors. Death from falling and from being crushed beneath collapsing scaffolding was a constant concern of painters, some of whom took it upon themselves to customize the structures they depended on. Leonardo, for example, designed

As his patron family looks on, a Renaissance artist applies a charcoal outline to a wall, the first step in creating a fresco.

his own custom-made scaffold that he could raise and lower with ropes while he was working on it. The design and construction of scaffolding was a matter of intimate concern to anyone depending on it for support high above stone floors.

Painters sometimes died from falls and from collapsing scaffolding. The most well-known master to fall and survive was Michelangelo, who seriously injured his legs but managed to return to finish the fresco. Known to work for several days at a time without climbing down, Michelangelo admitted to experiencing nausea and partial blindness from paint dripping in his eyes. He further injured his eyes because he insisted on working at night with only the light from a candle balanced in the cap he wore. Vasari describes Michelangelo's difficulties: "He worked under great personal inconvenience, constantly looking upwards so that he seriously injured his eyes. For months afterwards he could only read a letter when he held it above his head." [56]

UNUSUAL CONDITIONS

The many anonymous assistant painters who worked on large frescoes were generally treated poorly. Ghirlandaio was once invited to the nearby town of San Gimignano to oversee a large work for the abbey of Passignano. When the famed master arrived, the dozen or so assistants told Ghirlandaio of their ill treatment and poor-quality food. The evening of Ghirlandaio's arrival, the assistants assumed that the food would improve because the abbot would not wish to offend Ghirlandaio by providing his assistants with poor food. Nevertheless, the same coarse meat and foul porridge was served. The assistants responded by beating the monk in charge of food with a loaf of hard stale bread and dousing him in putrid porridge. When the abbot heard the commotion and came running to protect his monk, one of Ghirlandaio's assistants told the abbot that his master's talents "were worth more than all the abbots who ever lived in the monastery." [57] Recognizing his error, the abbot provided better meals after the food rebellion.

Problems of a technical nature also arose. Painting frescoes could become a haphazard undertaking because of the walls to be painted. None of the walls were in the same condition because of factors such as composition, thickness, moisture content, and texture. Usually, when a painter first arrived at the site of a fresco, considerable time and effort was spent on preparing the wall and customizing the paint to adhere to it. Leonardo da Vinci was a fearless experimenter who could spend more time on testing unusual pigments and varnishes than actually painting. According to Vasari, Leonardo received a commission for a painting from Pope Leo and immediately began to distill oils and herbs and

❧ DRESSING WHEN AWAY FROM THE *BOTTEGA* ❧

Whenever master painters worked in the villa of a wealthy patron, dress became a concern. What they wore often made a statement about their personalities, sense of individuality, and whether they would be invited back. Sometimes what the painters wore created as much gossip on the streets and in the villas of the Florentine upper class as their art did. For others, elegant dress guaranteed them access to the homes of the wealthy and allowed them to socialize in elegant style.

Painters could express themselves more flamboyantly in their dressing habits than sculptors, who spent most of their day pounding hammers on chisels while standing in the midst of flying pieces of stone and breathing marble dust. Leonardo, who rarely dabbled in sculpture, made the observation that a painter "sits before his work at the greatest of ease, well dressed and applying delicate colors with his light brush, and may dress himself in whatever clothes he pleases." Cennini expresses a similar view in his *Craftsman's Handbook:* "And let me tell you that doing a panel is really a gentleman's job, for you may do anything you want to with velvets on your back."

Some Florentine painters believed that by dressing in elegant robes, capes, and mink-trimmed coats, they could increase their chances for being hired to paint a fresco or portrait at the homes of the nobility. Vasari tells a story about the painter Dello Delli who preferred working in brocade, a rich oriental silk fabric with raised patterns in gold and silver. According to Vasari, Delli "could work and live like a noble, always painting in an apron of brocade." Vasari goes on to say that when Delli returned to Florence, he "rode to his house on horseback, . . . clothed with brocade."

Not every painter felt the need to dress like the rich in order to curry favor with them. One of the greatest painters of the Renaissance, if not the greatest, Michelangelo, never wore elegant clothing. He was known to work in old tattered shirts covered with paint and would often go weeks without bathing or changing his clothes. Masaccio was another who cared little about his clothing, as Vasari recorded: "[Masaccio] was very absent-minded and happy-go-lucky, his whole attention and will being devoted exclusively to his art, and he paid little attention to himself and less to others. He never took any heed or gave a thought to the cares or affairs of the world, not even about his clothes."

experiment on the varnish, whereupon the pontiff remarked, "Alas, this man will do nothing at all, since he is thinking of the end before he has made a beginning." [58]

LOCATING MATERIALS AWAY FROM HOME

Working away from home in an unfamiliar town and working for unfamiliar people often created problems that would not likely arise in Florence. Once when Perugino was away from Florence working on a commission requiring ultramarine blue, the most difficult pigment to find and the most expensive to purchase, the person paying for the commission provided Perugino with a pigment maker. The mixer was good at his craft, but he did not trust Perugino with the expensive pigment and insisted on doling it out in minute quantities and being present to ensure that the out-of-town painter did not steal it for use on another commission.

Insulted by such an obvious distrust for the master painter, Perugino took revenge on the man commissioning the painting. Instead of using the rare and expensive pigment, Perugino, by sleight of hand, hid the pigment in a cloth bag and applied none to the wall. Finally, when the fresco was done, the pigment maker realized that all of the ultramarine blue was gone but none could be seen in the painting. Perugino tricked the man a second time by telling him that the rare color had been absorbed into the plaster wall. As he was departing after completing the fresco, Perugino turned to the villa owner, handed him the cloth bag, and said, "This belongs to you; learn to trust honest men who would not deceive those who confide in them, though they might circumvent distrustful persons like yourself." [59]

Vibrant color was a hallmark of Michelangelo's art. When he was away from Florence painting the Sistine ceiling at the Vatican in Rome, his figures needed to be larger than life-size to be seen easily from the floor, one hundred feet below. To execute such an undertaking that would ultimately cover fifty-eight hundred square feet, Michelangelo

Outside the studio, master painters such as Perugino had to be shrewd businessmen.

needed unprecedented quantities of paint. In need of strong reds and yellows, and frustrated by not being able to buy them or dig them from the hills as he might in Florence, Michelangelo is said to have found a gardener's shovel that he used to probe the pope's garden for soils containing the pigments he needed.

SEPARATION FROM FAMILY AND FRIENDS

Not all fresco painters traveled with their entire family. Thus, working away from home, family, and friends often placed an emotional strain on painters. Without regular time for family and friends, painters sometimes became

For young master artists inspired by love, such as Raphael (shown here with the subject of his painting La Fornarina), *patrons occasionally had to pay to have loved ones join them on distant commissions.*

moody and melancholy, causing distractions from their work.

Raphael, for instance, had been commissioned to paint a first-floor interior for a prominent banker in Siena named Agostino Chigi. After Raphael had been at work for a short time, he began to miss a woman he was in love with and departed many times from Siena to visit her. When Chigi began to wonder if the painting would ever be completed, he sent house servants to visit the woman with a message to pack her belongings and move into his palace with Raphael until the commission was completed.

Others such as Fra Filippo Lippi, who was known to be a very sensual man with a reputation for stopping at nothing to satisfy his urges, often painted or drew the woman of his desire when he could not have the woman herself. When Lippi was commissioned to paint a picture for Cosimo de Medici in his villa, he was so distracted by the pleasures to be found in Florence that no painting got done. Finally, after repeated warnings, Cosimo locked Lippi in the villa. Not to be deterred, however, Lippi made a rope by tying bed sheets together and escaped back to the carnal pleasures of Florence. Cosimo sent his bodyguards after him and when they brought him back, Lippi finished the painting. Yet, as Vasari, who tells this story, concluded, "Painters are not beasts of burden." [60]

Whether Renaissance painters were viewed as beasts of burden by wealthy patrons or as creators, their social status was based on the individual relationships between members of the two groups. Without a doubt, each was dependent on the other to achieve their individual goals.

CHAPTER 5

PATRONS AND PAINTERS

Renaissance artists painted either custom works commissioned by wealthy secular and religious leaders or large quantities of mass-produced works intended for the middle-class market. Custom commissions could take years to design and complete. Such large works were accompanied by equally large price tags that could cause all but the wealthiest to wince, and even they winced from time to time. Fortunately for Florence and its esteemed coterie of painters, three distinct groups of art patrons financed the paintings that kept hundreds of artists employed. The affluent Catholic Church financed the decoration of churches and monasteries, aristocratic families paid for the beautification of civic buildings and their large stately villas, and the middle class paid for humble decorations for hundreds of small private homes.

THE CHURCH

Artistic fame was extended exclusively to those who executed important commissions for important patrons, and during the Renaissance none was more important than the collective economic clout of the many popes, cardinals, and bishops of the Catholic Church. The money that was gathered each Sunday on the collection plates was lavishly spent on paintings to decorate the many altars and church and monastery ceilings; portraits of church leaders; and religious icons.

Vasari pointed this out when discussing the life of painters such as Michelangelo who worked almost exclusively for popes and Antonio Pollaiuolo who, "had the patronage of rich pontiffs."[61] Money seemed to flow easily between these upper-crust ecclesiastical patrons and their painters. The money was a major attraction to painters but it was the power and authority of the church that accorded popes, cardinals, and archbishops preferential treatment over wealthy families. At this time in much of Europe, the Catholic Church was the most influential institution and no one dared offend any of its hierarchy. Contracts from the time indicate an enormous volume of art produced by Florentine painters for the church. Virtually every major painter produced at least one major commission for the church, many produced multiple works, and a few passed their entire lives in its employ. Most art historians accept the estimate that more than half of the paintings produced in Renaissance Florence were commissioned by the church.

PROBLEMS WORKING WITH THE CHURCH

In spite of the seemingly limitless supply of money, working for the church created unique problems. Unlike painting for wealthy families, popes and cardinals possessed the authority

In this fifteenth-century painting, clergy and religious patrons examine exterior frescos on a church. Such adornment became the hallmark of a Renaissance painter's career.

to demand paintings whether the artist wished to execute them or not. On several occasions, painters were ordered by church leaders to abandon commissions for private individuals in favor of projects for the church. Although such absolute authority is credited with generating the finest collection of Renaissance art in the world, it also greatly stressed the relationships between the church and various artists.

Michelangelo understood better than anyone did the tricky and often turbulent nature of papal patronage. Arguments between him and the pope were legendary. Vasari recorded one argument that pushed the relationship to the breaking point. One day, Michelangelo needed to speak with Pope Julius but the pope's personal attendant refused to allow him to be disturbed. Michelangelo, incensed at being dismissed by a mere attendant, said to him, "Tell his Holiness, when next he should inquire for Michelangelo that he had gone elsewhere." [62] Michelangelo was not a man known to bluff. He immediately sold his belongings and departed on horseback for Florence. Eventually, the authority of the pope prevailed, forcing Michelangelo to return.

Michelangelo had many other confrontations with Julius, in part because both men possessed pompous personalities and in part because both revered art. Julius was the greatest art patron within the papal line, commissioning many of the masterpieces of Renaissance art in Rome that included Michelangelo's Sistine Chapel, his marble statue *Moses,* and a barrage of dozens of paintings and frescoes by Raphael and Bramante.

When the pope offered the job of painting the ceiling of the Sistine Chapel to Michelangelo, the great painter suggested to the pope that Raphael would be a better choice and even went so far as to insist that he, Michelangelo, was really a sculptor, not a painter. Yet, as Vasari tells the story, "The more he refused, the more the impetuous pope insisted. When Michelangelo finally saw that the pope was determined, he resolved to accept the task." [63] This sort of arm-twisting took its toll on Michelangelo, who once confided his resentment toward the pope in what some art historians describe as an overly dramatic letter to a friend:

> Here I am, having lost my whole youth chained to this tomb [church] . . . and my excessive loyalty which is unrecognized is my ruin. Such is my fate. I see many people with an income of two or three thousand *scudi* [an Italian coin] remain in bed, and I, with the greatest labor, toil at impoverishing myself. [64]

Besides placing pressure on painters to conform their creative energies to the demands of the church, ecclesias-

❧ EXCUSES TO AVOID WORK ❧

Painters were sometimes so frustrated with their work that they were willing to do or say anything to escape a commission forced on them. The most notorious example of reluctance on the part of a painter was a commission for Michelangelo to paint the Sistine Chapel ceiling. Michelangelo first tried to avoid the work by repeatedly telling the pope that painting was not his artistic forte; sculpture was. When that failed, Michelangelo insisted that Raphael could execute a finer fresco. When that too failed, according to Ascenio Condivi in his biography The Life of Michelangelo,

When he [Michelangelo] had completed the picture of *The Flood*, it began to

mildew so that the figures could barely be distinguished. Therefore, Michelangelo reckoning that this must be a sufficient excuse for him to escape such a burden, went to the Pope and said to him, "Indeed I told your Holiness that this was not my art; what I have done is spoiled, and if you do not believe it, send someone to see." The Pope sent San Gallo, who when he saw it, realized that Michelangelo had applied the plaster too wet and consequently the dampness coming through produced that effect; and, when Michelangelo had been advised of this, he was forced to continue, and no excuse served.

Michelangelo meets with Pope Julius, who commissioned his work in the Sistine Chapel.

tical leaders sometimes acted as a censorship board. During the Renaissance, the Catholic Church was the single most powerful institution in Italy, as well as the wealthiest. The combination of the church's moral authority and economic strength determined the subject matter of most paintings. Almost all early Renaissance art and much of late Renaissance art reflected the religious and social values of the church. Censorship in the arts included controlling what subjects would be accept-

able to paint and how they could be depicted.

Painters such as Paolo Veronese, for example, who dared to paint an established conventional scene such as the Last Supper in an unconventional style, learned that such an offense could be costly. Veronese's painting of the well-known event included a dog, a man with a bloody nose, a man holding a green parrot, and a disciple cleaning his teeth with a toothpick. Because of his irreverent depiction of the Last Supper,

The inclusion of such mundane figures as dogs, goats, and jesters in religious paintings such as Veronese's The Wedding at Cana, *was not always received well by the church.*

Veronese was summoned to an inquisition and was

> obliged to improve and change his painting within a period of three months . . . and that all corrections should be made at the expense of the painter and that if he did not correct the picture he would be liable to the penalties imposed by the Holy Tribunal.[65]

PROBLEMS WORKING WITH ARISTOCRATS

It was not only offending the church that painters worried about. They also had problems with private patrons. Some patrons mistreated painters by cheating them and sometimes refusing to pay the agreed-on amount for a painting. One such patron, Agnolo Doni, agreed to pay Michelangelo sixty gold ducats for a small painting of Jesus, Mary, and Joseph. When the portrait was done, Michelangelo sent a messenger to collect the sixty ducats. Doni, however, sent the messenger back with only forty ducats, at which time Michelangelo sent the messenger back to Doni with a note to pay the sixty ducats or return the painting. What then occurred, as recorded by Vasari, was most interesting: "Doni at once offered the sixty as first demanded. But Michelangelo, offended, now demanded one hundred and forty, and so compelled him to pay more than double."[66]

Master painters were sometimes forced to endure the ignorance of wealthy art patrons who may have known a great deal about making money but very little about quality paintings. G.B. Armenini, a second-rate sixteenth-century painter, was astute enough to recognize ridiculous requests from patrons when he heard them. In a letter to a friend, he recounted being invited by another painter to review designs for a ceiling of a private villa. While the two painters stood in the villa reviewing the ornate drawings and discussing the placement of major figures, the patron suddenly approached the two painters. When one painter asked him what subjects he would like to see on the ceiling, the patron replied:

> "Make it [the fresco] like a pair of those trousers that are now so fashionable with many colors." This remark left the young man half stunned and I went away at once without saying anything. I decided, once I had taken leave, that I had better not go again.[67]

Other patrons such as Piero de Medici could be openly insulting. Piero, who had little respect for artists in general and hardly any for Michelangelo, once belittled him in front of his friends when he ordered the young master to sculpt a snowman in the courtyard of the Medici Palace following an unusually heavy snowstorm.

◆ THE ARISTOCRACY ◆

Florence was fortunate to be the home of a small but wealthy nucleus of prominent families whose fortunes from banking and international trading were spent on conspicuously large and ornate frescoes and family portraits. Rulers and other aristocratic families commissioned works of art from the most famous painters of the time to gain prestige over their social peers and advantages over political rivals. Socially prominent Florentines relished conversations at social gatherings where they heard the name or names of painters who had decorated their villas and their local churches. Nothing at this time brought more social status than owning a painting or fresco by one of the master artists of Florence. Occasionally, wealthy bankers and merchants were content to receive payment in art rather than gold florins or ducats.

Wealthy Florentine families paying imperial sums for large frescoes frequently asked for more than just the painting. Commissions of biblical scenes or frescoes depicting Greek and Roman leaders and members of the intelligentsia needed faces even though no one living during the Renaissance could possibly know what these famous people actually looked like. To satisfy the large egos of those paying the costs of equally large frescoes, the artists would use the faces of family members in the commission. Such a tradition, which became common-place, brought fame and prestige to members of leading families when their friends, as well as ordinary Florentine citizens, saw their faces prominently displayed on paintings that might last for hundreds of years.

Many of the great master painters understood their obligation to indulge wealthy patrons. Leonardo, for example, while painting the crucifixion, used the faces of Duke Ludovico and his eldest son for onlookers in the left foreground and his wife, the duchess Beatrice, and another son in the right foreground. The Medicis appear on dozens of paintings and frescoes, as Vasari attests in discussing a painting of the adoration of the Christ child that depicts members of the Medici family.

An occasional fringe benefit of working for wealthy patrons was their willingness to act as parents to young painters and employers of their parents. When Michelangelo was fifteen, for example, Lorenzo de Medici discovered the talents of the young man and wanted him to move into his villa while he was painting there. Since Michelangelo was still young, Lorenzo asked for and received permission from Michelangelo's father, Lodovico. According to Vasari, "Michelangelo stayed there four years, until the death of Lorenzo, receiving for himself an allowance of money and a purple cloak to wear, while his father, Lodovico, was made an official of the customs."

There was also the lurking possibility that a commissioned work might fail to please the patron. Many eminent painters dealt with disappointing reviews of their works, even Michelangelo. He had finished a canvas paining called *Leda and the Swan* for Duke Alfonso, but when Michelangelo delivered the painting expecting to be paid, the duke had instructed his personal attendant to handle the transaction. When the attendant saw the painting, he referred to it as merely a frivolous work. Stupefied by the attendant's ignorant comment, Michelangelo asked the man his profession, and when he said that he was a merchant, Michelangelo picked up his painting, placed it under his arm, and commented as he departed, "Indeed, then you are about to make a bad bargain for your master."[68] That painting, instead of being in the duke's personal collection, found its way into the collection of the king of France.

Piero de Medici, along with other members of his family, was an important patron of many Renaissance artists.

THE CITY OF FLORENCE

Dozens of cities dotting the Italian peninsula competed for the distinction of being considered the artistic and cultural center of Italy. To capture such an unofficial civic title, cities such as Pisa built a complex of buildings that included a bell tower that developed an unintentional yet distinctive lean. Venice built its own bell tower and cathedral set on a string of sinking islands. Rome, of course, was another obvious contender with the Vatican and centuries of Roman architecture.

Florence, however, unlike its rivals, countered with both an impressive array of civic architecture and paintings. In fact, no city could hope to compete with Florence's collection of paintings. The city council proclaimed that the expenditure of public revenues on the arts would greatly contribute *"ad urbis honorem et magnificentiam,"*[69] to the honor and glory of the city. Florentine citizens led by aristocratic families, guilds, government officials, and other influential civic organizations lent their support.

Money flowed into the pockets of the city's painters from a variety of civic sources. Several paintings decorating public buildings were paid for by fines imposed on dishonest businessmen. Others were paid for by levying a special tax for the reconstruction and beautification of important buildings, both public and private, such as Santo Spirito following a fire in 1471. An unusual inducement offered to the masters, such as Michelangelo, was a generous pension if they would retire in the city. Guilds were another source of funding for elaborate paintings to decorate their guildhalls. Everyone in Florence poured money into the pockets of the greatest painters to proudly proclaim Florence the capital of Renaissance art.

THE MIDDLE CLASSES

Only a select handful of accomplished virtuosos could expect princely incomes derived from commissioned masterpieces. Even though the popularity of paintings grew dramatically toward the middle of the fifteenth century, the other master painters counted themselves fortunate to have one or two masterpieces they could point to, for others had none at all. The majority of painters relied on hundreds of middle-income families and tourists purchasing small inexpensive works to keep their small workshops active. Middle-class patrons made many small investments in paintings to decorate and lend prestige to their modest homes. Most painters learned to keep their shop doors open by producing simpler, smaller, and less expensive paintings aimed at middle-income connoisseurs.

In order to make money on inexpensive art, owners of workshops focused on regularity and control of art rather than inspiration and genius.

⚜ THE MEDICI ⚜

No Florentine family played a more significant role as Renaissance art patrons than the wealthy Medici. As patrons to dozens of artists, this family acquired the most impressive collection of Renaissance paintings, frescoes, buildings, and statuary of any single entity (with the exception of the popes).

The origins of the House of the Medici and its fortune can be traced back to 1378 when the farming family moved to Florence to try their skills at banking. As the family successfully expanded its fortune, Giovanni de Medici (1360–1429) became known for his generosity as the first patron of the arts, helping Masaccio and paying for the reconstruction of the Basilica of San Lorenzo out of his own pocket. Giovanni had two sons, Cosimo (1389–1464) and Lorenzo (1395–1440), both of whom carried on their father's support for the arts and even expanded on it to become the most famous of their family for generosity toward the arts.

Cosimo spent lavishly on charitable acts, education, and art. He amassed the largest library in Europe and brought in many Greek sources, including the works of Plato, from Constantinople. The artists supported by Cosimo included Ghiberti, Brunelleschi, Donatello, Alberti, Fra Angelico, and Uccello. During his rule and that of his sons and grandson, Florence became the cultural center of Europe. Cosimo's son Piero (1416–1469) ruled for just a few years but continued his father's patronage of the arts.

Following the death of Piero came the rule of his son Lorenzo, who became known as "Lorenzo the Magnificent." Of all the Medici leaders, Lorenzo was the most acclaimed patron, commissioning noted painters such as Botticelli, Michelangelo, and Giovanni Pico della Mirandola.

While the Medici family was predominant, Florence was the cultural center of Europe. Although the family greatly influenced Florence's political and economic history, it is their patronage of the arts that led to the artistic beautification of the city that has become their lasting legacy.

Inexpensively produced artwork intended for the middle class was produced en masse by apprentices and assistants to keep the cost down. It was common for a master to design several popular, universal themes such as biblical stories and landscapes and then to execute hundreds of each theme. The favorite mediums of paintings purchased by middle-class art lovers were wood-panel diptychs and triptychs, which could be folded up on hinges for easy and safe transportation home on horseback or carts.

Grand Florentine festivals, like the one depicted in this fifteenth-century painting, were the ideal venue for artists, who roamed through the crowds or set up booths to sell their works and advertise their talents.

Selling to the public was simplified by not requiring contracts but was complicated by advertising the products. In addition to displaying inexpensive paintings on the sidewalks outside of the *botteghe,* painters also sent their older apprentices to city festivals with cartloads of paintings to sell to the throngs enjoying the merriment. Festivals, both religious and secular, added a great deal of color and drama to the life of Florence. As many as forty a year were carefully choreographed there. Visitors wandering the many booths could find an excellent array of paintings costing one florin or less.

Most masters could not afford to turn down work, however simple. Ghirlandaio, the master of one of the largest and most prestigious *botteghe* in Florence, had so many apprentices to pay and so many materials to purchase that he told his apprentices to accept every commission brought to the shop. To stress the importance of accepting all work, even if it meant painting women's baskets, he told his apprentices that "if they would not paint them, he would do them himself—no one was to be sent away unsatisfied." [70]

CHAPTER 6

ART AS A BUSINESS

Conducting the business of painting masterpieces was as much an art form as the actual painting. To the uneducated eye, the ornately painted frescoes that colorfully decorated the stately villas and venerable churches of Florence belied the hard-nosed negotiations and sweat that made the masterpieces possible. Far removed from idyllic notions of painting cathedral ceilings and portraits of the rich and famous, master painters had business responsibilities that required as much of their time and skills as their art did.

Master painters could not afford to lose money on their commissions. *Botteghe* owners were businessmen required to pay wages to apprentices, purchase expensive art supplies, pay rent on their shops, submit bids on major works, and fulfill tax obligations. Failure to keep a keen eye on finances could end a career in the high-

ly competitive business of painting. Artisans learned from experience how to attract customers and how to elevate their painting styles above those of their competitors in order to secure further contracts and to increase their compensation.

THE POWER OF THE GUILDS

The painting profession in Florence was loosely regulated by its guild, the *Medici e Speziali,* doctors and specialists. In addition to doctors and painters, it was also the guild of pharmacists and spice dealers, both of which sold minerals and spices to the doctors to make medicines and to the painters to make paint pigments.

Virtually all professions during the Renaissance were organized into guilds within each city. Guilds were formal associations of workers that protected their workers from outside competition and assured fair wages for their members. In addition to these protective measures, guilds also functioned as fraternal organizations to provide some financial support for widows and orphans and to pay for a workman's burial.

The largest guilds in Florence were the bakers, weavers, butchers, leatherworkers, and armor makers. Artists also had their own individual guilds, for sculptors, architects, goldsmiths, and painters of wood panels, linen, and canvas. Anyone in Florence who wished to practice as a painter and sell his works was obligated to join one of the many artist guilds. The members were compelled to pay an annual membership fee whether they liked it or not, and many did not. Michelangelo complained about having to hand over dues to the art guild in Florence, and Brunelleschi was heavily fined for falling in arrears for several years.

For the highly sought-after Florentine masters, the painters' guild played a minimal role, if any at all. For the dozens of

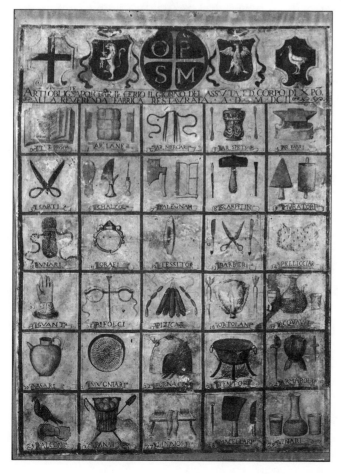

A painting illustrates just a few of the many guilds in Renaissance Florence, each represented by a particular symbol.

struggling lesser-known painters and their apprentices, however, the guild played a significant role in keeping them in business. Many of the small churches in and around Florence, for example, sought painters to decorate their altars but had little money to spend on such undertakings. The art guild matched wealthy patrons with small churches to finance the work and made sure that only deserving painters with modest incomes were given the work.

Guilds also protected the integrity of their members by overseeing the quality of their paintings. They had a list of rules governing the quality of work and the integrity of all business transactions. Guild inspectors could examine the quality of work and make recommendations for changes if the quality failed to meet their standards. Guild rules also protected patrons from being overcharged by occasional unscrupulous members. Guilds also enforced contracts between masters and apprentices and had the authority to revoke membership if any member incurred too many infractions or refused to rectify improper business practices.

GIFTS TO WEALTHY ART COLLECTORS

The wealth of businessmen and clerics was the economic engine that powered Renaissance painting. Without the wealthy, the art of Renaissance Florence might fit in a single small obscure museum rather than filling many

of the world's most prestigious museums. This fact, which was as obvious five hundred years ago as it is today, prompted many master painters to influence the rich in ways they did not for middle-class art patrons, since currying the favor of a few influential men was the foundation for their artistic and financial success.

Presenting gifts of art to wealthy collectors was one of the tactics used by painters to gain and hold the attention of potential buyers. Some artists believed that by making a gift to a wealthy art buyer, they would gain fame by having their paintings seen hanging alongside better-known painters. Other artists bestowed paintings on influential collectors with the hope that their expression of generosity might create an obligation on the part of the collectors to purchase pieces in the future or to barter for something else of value.

Late in life, Mantegna sent a painting he had executed of St. Sebastian to a bishop of the Catholic Church. After hearing nothing from the bishop except for his verbal expression of appreciation, Mantegna conveyed his disappointment to him in this letter:

> When I presented the little picture to your Grace last Sunday, you responded flatteringly and with a degree of pleasure in your countenance, saying that you would be pleased to give me a parcel of land. [71]

❧ SALARIES FOR PAINTERS ☙

How much money Renaissance painters received for their works was determined by many factors. Most prominent were the reputation of the painter, the patron, and the size and difficulty of the commission. Frescoes, for example, were far more costly because of their size, degree of difficulty (requiring the preparation of the wall), and the additional expense of having to employ several *garzoni* to assist in the large undertaking. The largest frescoes cost one hundred times more than the largest canvas paintings.

During the Renaissance, Italians and most Europeans used either the gold Venetian ducat or the gold Florentine florin, each weighing 3.5 grams. With the exception of bartering for the services of a painter, contracts stipulated payment in either of the two equally valued coins.

In 1481, Ghirlandaio was paid twelve hundred gold ducats for a large fresco that took four years to complete; in ad-

dition, he received another two hundred ducats because the patron was so happy with the completed work. Three years later, however, Vasari claims that Ghirlandaio received a commission to execute a combination of a fresco and a mosaic in the city of Siena for twenty thousand ducats. Unfortunately, Ghirlandaio died before it was completed.

Michelangelo executed a small canvas painting early in his career for sixty ducats. His most esteemed fresco, which he painted on the Sistine Chapel ceiling between 1508 and 1512, cost the pope fifteen thousand ducats. Although it is unclear how much of this amount Michelangelo received, it is likely that he got most of it.

As a point of comparative value for painters' incomes, Raphael's exquisite villa in Rome cost him the princely sum of three thousand ducats, and Michelangelo's contract as an apprentice averaged eight florins a year plus room and board.

A front (left) and back view of a fifteenth-century Florin.

Obviously, Mantegna was anticipating something more than flattery in exchange for the painting. The parcel of land referred to in the letter never materialized, but such bartering of goods was not unusual.

Gifts of paintings to influence patrons often backfired. Botticelli received nothing in return for his gift of his *Calumny of Apelles* to the influential Florentine Antonio Segni. Leonardo da Vinci also received no benefit when he gave a drawing of Neptune to Segni.

BEAUTIFYING THE ORDINARY

Part of the Renaissance spirit in Florence was its fervor for taking the ordinary and beautifying it. In pursuing this passion, Renaissance masters painted more than canvases and frescoes. Their exceptional skills were often called on to beautify many mundane objects such as shields and helmets, parade banners, wagons, saddles, beds, storage chests, dinner plates, and even draperies.

One of the more interesting stories about the venerable Leonardo da Vinci described a badly damaged wood shield owned by a wealthy man who wished to have it repainted. When the shield arrived in Leonardo's *bottega,* he sent it to a woodworker to smooth the surface so that he could then paint the fearsome and hideous head of Medusa, whose face was said to paralyze with fear anyone who saw it. Leonardo became so engrossed in this simple project that

when the owner arrived to take the shield home, Leonardo darkened the room and placed the shield where a dim light would strike it. When the owner saw the grisly face, according to Vasari, "he drew back, startled, and turned to rush out, but Leonardo stopped him and said, 'the shield will serve its purpose.'" [72]

Painters also used their skills on parade banners and floats. Florentines loved parades celebrating religious holidays, the arrival of foreign dignitaries, and a variety of local traditions. The floats that were pulled through the

A young da Vinci hangs back as his startled patron encounters the artist's terrifying and realistic image of Medusa on a shield.

❧ A PLEA FOR MORE MONEY ❧

A few patrons paid all fresco painters the same rate without regard for their ability or reputation. Payment was based on a flat rate for the amount of square feet painted. In 1450, the painter Francesco del Cossa appealed to a duke to increase his pay because of his superior abilities. Art historian Creighton Gilbert provides the following letter from Cossa to the duke in his book Italian Art, 1400–1500.

Most illustrious Prince and Excellent Lord. I am Francesco del Cossa, who has made by myself the three wall sections towards the entry room. And so illustrious lord, if your lordship wishes to give me no more than ten pennies per foot, . . . it gives me great pain and grief within me. Especially considering that I,

when after all I have begun to have a little of a name [reputation], should be treated and judged, and compared to the sorriest assistants. And that my having studied, and I study all the time, should not at this point have a little more reward, and especially from your lordship, than a person who had avoided such study. And because my work proves what I have done, and I have used gold and good colors, if they were of the same value as those who have gone ahead without such labor it would surprise me.

Following this dramatic plea for more money, the duke replied to Cossa, saying by way of an aide, "Let him be content with the fee that was set, for it was set for those chosen for the individual fields."

streets were often ornately designed and painted to reflect the city's passion for decorative art. Very often, several of the floats were painted by the city's most talented painters. One such artist, Piero di Cosimo, decorated a float celebrating the arrival of the pope that was draped in black and painted with morbid scenes such as skeletons and ghosts rising from graves. In spite of the ghoulish images, spectators who saw it described it as being "novel and terrifying . . . yet it brought high praise to Piero and set a fashion for this sort of display in Florence where such pag-

eants were produced as were never equaled by any other city." [73]

COMMISSIONS AND CONTRACTS

Agreements between early Renaissance painters and patrons consisted of little more than a brief verbal description of the painting to be produced and a handshake. Contracts were largely unnecessary because the paintings were restricted to a narrow band of biblical depictions such as the birth of Christ, the crucifixion, and the resurrection. These oft-repeated subjects were so commonly seen and so similar that requesting an artist to paint any one of them was simply a matter of specifying size, material, cost, and completion date. When the church or a private party requested a painting of a crucifixion, for example, they knew what to expect, and few were disappointed.

Giotto ended the monotony of art with fresh ideas, thus introducing the need for written contracts. As the Renaissance moved forward, Giotto and his protégés represented the old common themes in styles, colors, and interpretations never before imagined. Such an upheaval in painting meant that patrons could be certain of the end product only if everything was carefully specified in writing. Lengthy contracts stipulated the subject, painting style, amount of detail, expressions on faces, colors to be used and their location, painting size, date of completion, price, late penalties, and myriad other details to ensure that both parties got what they agreed to.

An example of a contract mired in detail was the one between the painter Matteo di Giovanni and the bakers guild in 1478 that, among dozens of other things, specified these three items:

Item, in the middle of the aforementioned panel the figure of St. Barbara is to be painted, sitting in a golden chair and dressed in a robe of crimson brocade. Item, in the said panel shall be painted two angels flying, showing that they are holding the crown over the head of St. Barbara. Item, on one side of St. Barbara, that is on the right, should be painted the figure of St. Catherine the German, and on the left the figure of St. Mary Magdalene.[74]

Even with the use of contracts, disagreements between artists and patrons occurred, sometimes causing the artist to quit in anger. In 1436, Jacopo della Quercia explained that he was quitting his work for officials at the church of San Petronio for not being paid:

The truth is this: that I have left your city and your reverent magistracy, not to walk out upon my obligation or depart from common reason, but to be free and not captive, because a captive man is neither heard nor understood. Your demands do not accord with my part of the contract drawn up in the past; your reverence knows it all and that it cannot take place. If you are willing to give me what is my due, I shall appear at once, . . . I shall wait three or four days for your reverences' reply. Should there be no reply, I shall take the road to Siena. Even, however, if our Lord God is willing to make good my deficit [the money owed me] he will not be able to remove all the malice.[75]

Sometimes artists were willing to sign contracts specifying low wages in exchange for other benefits. In 1503, the wool guild signed a contract with Michelangelo for a mere two florins a month to execute works that would take him an estimated twelve months. Such a monthly salary was ridiculously low, but Michelangelo also included in the contract a piece of land and the construction of a house built to his requirements.

CONTRIBUTIONS BY ASSISTANTS

Many master painters relied heavily on their assistants to help complete large commissions. Raphael, for example, was known to keep his assistants "working on them [cartoons] drawing

Matteo di Giovanni's St. Barbara Enthroned *was a painting restricted, in every detail, by a binding contract between artist and patron.*

from his drawings, and he inspected every part and did the more important parts himself." [76] Others, however, prided themselves in designing and executing large masterpieces entirely alone. The difference between the two camps for some painters was a sense of personal pride and commitment in performing all of the work; for others, it was a business decision aimed at producing as many works as possible in order to fatten their bank accounts.

Assistants performed many jobs for their master painters, which some-times included the design and execution of a complete work without ever disclosing the deception to the patron. One such painter known to have a reputation for high-quality works that exceeded his own ability was Bernardino Pinturicchio, who used many apprentices to complete his paintings. Pinturicchio's reputation for perpetrating this fraud prompted Vasari to label him among the undeserving by commenting about him, "Many of the undeserving are aided by fortune while numbers of able men have per-

This cartoon of Raphael's The School of Athens *was prepared by his assistants before the master artist painted his famous fresco in Rome.*

✑ ADVICE ON GOLD AND QUALITY PAINTING ✑

Cennini wrote his book The Craftsman's Handbook *not only as a primer on the execution of painting techniques but also as a treatise on painting fine-quality art. One of the more unusual techniques occasionally used on frescoes was the inclusion of gold leaf, actual pieces of paper-thin beaten gold. The gold leaf functioned to highlight important details because it reflected light, causing viewers to focus on it. In Cennini's treatise on the quality of gold leaf, he took the opportunity to remind painters to focus on producing high-quality works.*

Most people make a practice of embellishing a wall with golden tin, because it is less costly [than gold leaf]. But I give you this urgent advice, to make an effort always to embellish with fine gold, and with good colors, especially in the figure of Our Lady. And if you wish to reply that a poor person cannot make the outlay, I answer that if you do your work well, and spend time on your jobs, and good colors, you will get such a reputation that a wealthy person will come to compensate you for the poor one; and your standing will be so good for using good colors that if a master is getting one ducat for a figure, you will be offered two; and you will end by gaining your ambition. As the old saying goes, good work, good pay. And even if you were not adequately paid, God and Our Lady will reward you for it, body and soul.

sistent hard luck."[77] The fortune that Vasari referred to was Pinturicchio's good fortune to employ many able assistants, one of whom was the great Raphael, who emerged as the last brilliant Renaissance painter. When Pinturicchio was invited to Siena to paint the library of Pope Pius II, Vasari reported that "It is indeed true that all the cartoons for the stories were drawn by Raphael of Urbino."[78]

Too much involvement in major paintings by a master's assistants could become scandalous. The master most known to allow his assistants to perform on significant works was Raphael, who completed hundreds of major works. He turned so much of his work over to assistants that, toward the end of his life, complaints were circulating and many art enthusiasts were openly asking who had painted the latest Raphael painting.

As a young painter, Raphael executed the design and the outlines, leaving the rest of a fresco for his assistants. Later in his career, however, he was commissioned to paint so many frescoes simultaneously that he could not possibly have a hand in all of them. The uproar from rival painters and patrons became so acute that Vasari, a friend of Raphael, felt obligated to comment about Raphael's involvement in one large fresco: "For these pictures, Raphael prepared the cartoons and painted many of the figures with his own hand."[79]

Michelangelo's temperament and standards of perfection precluded the use of assistants. When he began to design the massive ceiling of the Sistine Chapel, he actually summoned two excellent master painters to assist him. Michelangelo designed and drew all of the figures, but he sought help filling in the figures because they were so large and there were so many. He gave each of the two painters a small test area to paint but was so unhappy with the results that he sent them away because their work was "far from approaching his expectations or fulfilling his purpose."[80]

STEALING FROM SUCCESSFUL MASTERS

Many painters, including the most creative, understood that copying the style of a successful artist could bring them success. For this reason, many painters executed works that could be confused with the works of others. Sometimes they took the copying of style and technique too far. Leonardo, who was not only a master painter but also a master student of art history, recognized the drawback of too much copying when he wrote, "After the time of Giotto the art of painting declined again because everyone imitat-

ed the pictures that were already done. Thus it went on from century to century until Tommaso, of Florence, nicknamed Masaccio."[81]

Although many painters, even the best, copied ideas and styles from their colleagues, none would ever admit to such underhanded foolishness. Still, such shameful thievery occurred unabashedly. Vasari tells the amusing story of the young Raphael who wanted desperately to view one of the frescoes that the older great master Michelangelo was painting. The problem Raphael faced was twofold: First, Michelangelo did not want anyone to see his work until he had completed it, and second, Michelangelo insisted on locking the room at all times. Raphael managed to get a key when Michelangelo was out of town and sneaked in. So moved was he by the wondrous figures that he saw that he departed and went directly to a fresco he had been working on. As Vasari writes,

Instantly, Raphael repainted the figure of the prophet Isaiah, which he had finished in the church of San Agostino, and in this work he profited so greatly by what he had seen in the work of Michelangelo that his manner was inexpressibly enlarged and received henceforth an obvious increase in majesty.[82]

Raphael was caught red-handed. Michelangelo, who had seen Raphael's figures before he altered them, railed at him for copying the figures he was privately painting. From that time on, Michelangelo ended his friendship with Raphael and never missed an opportunity to remind him to whom he owed his success.

Observing the contracts, transactions, and business shenanigans that took place among Renaissance painters as well as between them and their patrons, it is easy to conclude that the greatness of Renaissance

A fifteenth-century painting depicts artists carefully studying the work of Michelangelo.

Florence was truly the result of artistic ability rather than business acumen. This same observation seems to be equally true looking at the personal lives of the master painters. Although many of the lesser names managed lives of relative normalcy, a high percentage of the superstars found themselves caught in undercurrents that colored their personal lives but fortunately not their art.

CHAPTER 7

THE PRIVATE LIVES AND PERSONALITIES OF FLORENTINE PAINTERS

At the end of a workday, painters sent their *garzoni* home for the night, closed their *botteghe,* and went home to their families and friends just like most other workers in Florence. The majority of the city's hundreds of painters walking the cobblestone streets to their apartments at dusk made enough money to pay for their rent, food, and other necessities, but not much more. Relegated to painting mediocre works for tourists and middle-class patrons, these painters failed to attract the attention of the aristocrats and writers of the time such as Vasari. As a result of their obscure ordinary existences, little is known about their personal lives, as is the case with their fellow citizens who lived their lives as accountants, shopkeepers, tavern owners, and manual laborers.

Then there were the superstars of Florentine art. This handful of painters, whose collective genius was recognized and celebrated by prominent families and the Catholic Church, caught the attention of writers, who recorded not only their artistic achievements but their personal lives as well. When discussing the personal lives of Renaissance painters, it is done in the context of this small group of successful artisans.

SPENDING HABITS

Some Florentine Renaissance painters amassed sizable fortunes. Some of them spent money ostentatiously while pursuing their aspirations for acceptance into high social circles. These few lived handsomely, spending lavishly on sumptuous dinner parties, elegant fashionable clothes, and fabled villas on the hillsides of Florence as well as in metropolitan Rome.

Sandro Botticelli was one such painter who commanded huge commissions for his portraits of popes and

❧ CONDIVI ❧

Though a painter in his own right, Ascanio Condivi is best known as Michelangelo's biographer. He published his biography of Michelangelo, *The Life of Michelangelo,* in 1553, three years after Vasari published his biography of Michelangelo because the master took exception to some of the statements that Vasari made. Condivi's biography was therefore meant to correct much of what Vasari had said.

Condivi was a friend to Michelangelo and he writes not only from in-timate personal knowledge but at times almost at dictation from the master. Art historians consider Condivi's account of Michelangelo to be more accurate than that of Vasari. Although it is generally accepted that Condivi took liberties with Michelangelo's lineage, the chronology and details of the artist's working life are still held to be reliable. Condivi's work served as the basis for Vasari's later revisions in his 1568 edition of *The Lives of the Artists.*

Florentine aristocrats. According to Vasari, "He squandered [his fortune] on his residence in Rome, where he lived immoderately, as was his habit."[83] Botticelli was not the only Florentine to own a home in Rome. Raphael, at the age of thirty, was able to afford the famous Palazzo Caprini for the astronomical price of three thousand ducats. This elegant villa in the most fashionable district in Rome came to be known as the "House of Raphael" for years after he died.

Fellow Florentine Perugino was another who spent his money freely. Unlike Botticelli, however, Perugino was said to trust only in money and had a reputation for doing anything to get more of it. One of his weaknesses was elegant houses. According to Vasari, Perugino "became very rich and bought, as well as built, several great houses."[84]

Houses, clothes, and fine wines may have been the most common forms of indulgences, but they were not the only ones. Leonardo da Vinci, for example, was a known lover of fast horses, and he owned many. For some painters who did not marry, women could become a major expense, as was the case with Raphael, who, according to Vasari, "permitted himself to indulge too freely in the society of women."[85]

Some painters lived at the other end of the spectrum. These men made a great deal of money but tended to give it away since they had little concern for their appearance or where they slept. Masaccio, for example, whose real name was Tommaso, was known throughout Florence to be so focused on his paintings that he neglected all else. He was frequently seen roaming the streets in filthy old clothes and sleeping wherever it was convenient, often in barns and shop entryways. He was often disheveled and reeking of foul odors, and Vasari explains that it was this disregard for his person that earned him the nickname Masaccio, which means "filthy Tom." This disparaging nickname was used so often that it eventually replaced his real name.

A kindred spirit with Masaccio was Michelangelo, who was widely known for his bohemian lifestyle. He often wore one shirt and pair of pants for months at a time, even sleeping in them because it did not seem "worthwhile to

Raphael, seen here completing a commission at the Vatican, kept an elegant residence in Rome.

undress only to dress again the next morning."[86] While painting frescoes, he slept on top of his scaffolding to avoid wasting his time climbing up and down. Michelangelo's austere and unconventional lifestyle was unrelated to his personal wealth, which was great. His good friend Vasari asserted that "Although rich, he lived like a poor man and rarely had a guest at his table."[87]

ARROGANCE

Arrogance concerning one's painting abilities seemed to be a common trait

---

✑ LOATHING AMONG COLLEAGUES ✍

Animosity between master painters often took forms far more severe than casual insults. Historians such as Condivi and Vasari describe some relationships in viscious terms that suggest hatred. Michelangelo, for example, seemed to have difficulty nurturing any friendships with other artists. His enmity toward Raphael and Leonardo da Vinci was legendary; Michelangelo seemed incapable of walking the same streets with the other two men. Vasari was aware of the problem, commenting in his book *The Lives of the Artists,* "Michelangelo even left Florence because of it."

Jealousies and loathing among painters sometimes flared beyond reasonable limits. On several occasions, the painter Pietro Aretino asked Michelangelo to send him drawings that he was working on, but Michelangelo never paid any attention to the requests of the minor painter. Frustrated by what he viewed as Michelangelo's lack of respect and injured by not even having received a reply, Aretino attacked the great master in a letter that he promised to destroy but later released to the public. In the letter, reproduced in Robert Klein's book *Italian Art, 1500–1600,* Aretino falsely accused Michelangelo of violating a contract with the pope and went so far as to charge, "Your failure to discharge your obligations is reckoned to you as an act of thieving." To make his attack on Michelangelo even more viscious, Aretino added the false statement that he believed that the world would appreciate the suggestions he had made to Michelangelo for his fresco *The Last Judgment,* even though he would never receive credit for the suggestions.

Sometimes great artists allowed their obsessive resentment to overshadow their artistic focus. Andrea del Castagno, for example, was known throughout Florence for his inability to control his vengeful emotions toward his colleagues. Vasari said of him, "He buried his splendid talent under the rancor and envious hatred of his nature." According to Vasari, Castagno was known to gouge his fingernails into paintings of his rivals and even to start fistfights with them. The worst incident, however, was when he came across a painter and longtime acquaintance asleep on a street and seized the opportunity to beat him severely with a heavy weight.

among master painters. A few of them occasionally openly expressed their sense of artistic superiority, a characteristic that sometimes could irritate colleagues and patrons yet was rarely challenged. Sometimes expressions of arrogance could also be entertaining and comical.

A courtier from Pope Boniface VIII came to Giotto telling him that the pope wanted to make use of his services and asked him for a drawing that he could send to his holiness as proof of his superior talent. Without a moment's hesitation, Giotto took a sheet of paper and a brush dipped in red paint, positioned his arm to his side, and, with a twist of his hand, drew a perfect circle. Then, with a smile, he said to the courtier, "There's your drawing." As if he were being ridiculed, the courtier replied, "Is this the only drawing I'm to have?" "It's more than enough," answered Giotto. "Send it and you will see if its worth is recognized." [88] The messenger angrily departed but delivered the drawing to the pope nonetheless. As soon as the more experienced eyes of the pope settled on the drawing, he immediately perceived Giotto's superior skills.

One of the most arrogant statements recorded was that of Leonardo da Vinci, who, with no hesitation, recommended himself as the greatest living painter. When the wealthy art patron Ludovico Sforza asked him who he could recommend for a major commission, Leonardo recommended himself, asserting, "I can execute sculpture in marble, bronze, or clay, and also I can do in painting whatever any man can do, be he who he may." [89]

Even Michelangelo, normally known for his humility, could attack a colleague with bitter contempt for their work while expressing his own personal arrogance. In a letter he wrote expressing his anger at Raphael, Michelangelo concluded by arrogantly asserting, "Yet, Raphael had good reason to be jealous of me, for all he knew of art he learned from me." [90]

Arrogance might even take the unusual form of including one's own portrait in a painting. Raphael's most recognized fresco, *The School of Athens,* depicts thirty or so of the foremost thinkers of the Greek Golden Age. Centrally focused in the large fresco are the philosophers Plato and Aristotle surrounded by other illustrious Greek philosophers, mathematicians, geographers, and poets. Only the most revered intellects are represented. Yet far off to the right, where Raphael painted some onlookers, he could not resist the temptation to include himself in this august gathering. Many art historians analyzing this interesting anomaly have concluded that he believed his artistic genius qualified him to be in the company of the greatest thinkers, but not necessarily center stage.

ECCENTRIC BEHAVIOR

The eccentric behavior displayed by some Florentine painters became

Raphael, located in the foreground, second from far right in his painting The School of Athens, *could not resist the temptation to include himself among the world's most famous artists and thinkers.*

legendary both because of its bizarre nature and because of its comedy. Many of the more outlandish stories tended to be retold many times by bemused patrons as a form of entertainment.

The story recounted by Vasari about Piero di Cosimo and his eating habits is one harmless yet amusing story that gave credence to the common notion that many painters were indeed a strange lot. It seems that Cosimo spent so much of his time preparing glues and varnishes using an egg base that

He allowed himself no other food but hard-boiled eggs, and these he cooked only when he had a fire to boil his glues and varnishes. Nor did he cook them six or eight at a time, but by the fifties. He kept them in a basket and ate them when he was hungry. This mode of existence suited him perfectly; any other seemed to him the merest slavery.[91]

Animals seemed to be interesting diversions to a few painters. The house of the late Renaissance painter Il Sodoma was described by his friend Vasari as being "Like Noah's ark . . . with especially exotic or otherwise remarkable animal species: badgers, squirrels, small apes, Angora cats, bantams, turtle doves, etc." [92] Sodoma was not the only painter with an attraction for animals. Vasari also describes Leonardo's eccentric predilection for seeing beautiful exotic birds for sale as he strolled the streets of Florence; "he used to buy [the birds] to set them free." [93]

The eccentric sometimes escalated to the bizarre. Piero di Cosimo was known among his colleagues to isolate himself from others while living the life of a wild man. Rarely cutting his hair or bathing, he was sometimes seen on the streets of Florence searching for animals and plants to take home for his dinner. Vasari suggested that he was perhaps psychotic when saying that the ideas for many of his paintings came "from stains of filth thrown against a wall[;] he would conjure strange scenes, combats of horses, curious cities, and extraordinary landscapes." [94]

HUMOR

Humor was often used to soften stressful moments between impatient patrons and hot-tempered artists. The

Piero di Cosimo's Perseus Liberating Andromeda *is a wild scene with strange creatures and flying men. Many of di Cosimo's peers attributed his odd paintings to his eccentric way of life.*

❧ ACCEPTING CONSTRUCTIVE CRITICISM ❧

Criticism among painters was sometimes intended to convey nothing more than personal attacks lacking merit and so deserved to be dismissed with little serious consideration. Other times, however, the criticism was intended to convey constructive advice to assist painters in improving their works. Often, painters on the receiving end of the criticism did not know which was intended. In an attempt to encourage painters to listen carefully and to learn from criticism, Alberti proffered the following sage advice in his book On Painting.

Give to things a moderated diligence and take the advice of friends. In painting, open yourself to whoever comes and hear everyone. The work of the painter attempts to be pleasing to the multitude; therefore do not disdain the judgment and views of the multitude when it is possible to satisfy their opinions. They say that Apelles [an ancient Greek painter] hid behind a painting so that each one could more freely criticize it and so that he could hear their honest opinions: Thus he heard how each one blamed or praised. Hence I wish our painter openly to demand and to hear each one who judges him. This will be most useful to him in acquiring pleasantness. There is no one who does not think it an honor to pass judgment on the labors of others. It scarcely seems doubtful to me that the envious and detractors prejudice the fame of the painter. To the painter all his merits were always known, and the things which he has painted well are testimonies to his fame. Therefore, hear each one, but first of all have everything well thought out and well thrashed out with yourself. When you have heard each one, believe the most expert.

A 1511 painting by Giorgio Vasari of Greek artist Apelles hiding behind his painting in order to eavesdrop on his critics.

most common tension between patrons and artists was that of long-overdue commissions. Leonardo, who was once months behind delivering a painting depicting Christ and Judas, was observed by the duke paying for the painting to be passing many days in inactivity. Finally, the duke could no longer restrain his irritation at seeing no progress and summoned Leonardo to encourage him to finish the work. Leonardo calmly explained the difficulty of creating Christ's face because no one alive had seen it and the face required a special look of serenity and celestial grace. As for the face of Judas, it too required a special look; it needed to convey depravity, treachery, and betrayal. According to Vasari, Leonardo then hesitated and said to the duke that he "would still search but as a last resort he could use the head of a duke for that of Judas."[95] With that, the duke laughed, leaving Leonardo to complete the painting without further interruptions.

As Giotto's end drew near, his energy for work continued in spite of his declining health. King Robert of Naples invited him to his palace as a personal guest of the royal household in 1329. For the next four years, Giotto drew a monthly salary, a sum that must have been extravagant although it is not recorded. While in Naples, he painted several portraits of royalty and a few biblical scenes, all now lost. He created an enduring friendship with the king that was illustrated by a witty exchange

while he was painting outside during the oppressive late afternoon summer's heat. Sensing Giotto's frailty, King Robert said to him, "If I were you, I would quit for the afternoon." Hearing his comment, Giotto paused for a moment and snapped back, "And so would I, if I were you."[96]

TAUNTS AND BARBS

The small circle of elite painters in Florence competing for a limited number of commissions caused the cauldron of personal animosity to boil over on occasion. The tightly interwoven relations gave rise to fierce criticism of artistic merit and occasional face-to-face verbal confrontations. Fortunately for Renaissance art, the pressure of most personal animosity could be relieved by a few artfully chosen insults. Certain artists expressed personalities in direct conflict with others. Art historian Martin Wackernagel makes the point that "Vasari speaks of the painters' mutually malicious tongues as if a traditional characteristic of Florentine artistic society."[97]

Verbal barbs between two of the most revered Florentine painters, Michelangelo and Raphael, became legendary on the city's streets. One such exchange occurred when Michelangelo, known for his reclusive lifestyle, was walking to the Sistine Chapel alone when he encountered his artistic rival and social opposite Raphael in the company of a crowd of friends and admirers. Michelangelo shot out to him the intended insult, "Like a prince with his retinue." Not to be left without a retort, Raphael shot back, "And you, solitary like the hangman."[98]

The lively art of the insult against colleagues often involved criticism of paintings. The Renaissance painter and historian Paolo Pino related the story of one painter who showed his new work to another painter while boasting of how quickly he had executed it. Looking briefly at the canvas and being unimpressed, the friend replied, "You do not have to tell me, the work itself shows it."[99]

Vasari describes the cruelty that one painter could express toward another in recounting the chance meeting between Paolo Uccello and Donatello. Uccello had been hard at work for many months on a major painting for a church. While working on the masterpiece, he built a wood barrier around it so that no one could see the painting as it took form. On the day that Uccello revealed the completed work to the world, Donatello happened to go by, and when Uccello asked his more famous colleague for his opinion, Donatello crushed Uccello by saying, "Why! Paolo, you are uncovering your picture just when you should be shutting it from the sight of all."[100]

COMPLIMENTS TO FELLOW PAINTERS

On occasion, painters were capable of generous and genuine compliments. In 1490, a wealthy duke asked a painter who he might recommend for a painting and he replied,

Sandro di Botticelli, a most excellent painter in panel and fresco, his things have a manly air and also have very good organization and complete balance.

Filippino di Fra Filippo, very good, pupil of the above, and son of the most remarkable master of his time, his things have a gentler air, I don't think they have as much skill.

Perugino, an outstanding master, especially in fresco, his things have an angelic air, very gentle.

Domenico di Ghirlandaio, good master in panel and more in fresco, his things have a good air, and he is very expeditious and does a lot of work.[101]

HONORS IN DEATH

Death bestowed final honors upon many Florentine artists. As a final tribute reserved exclusively for the finest creative geniuses, funeral processions consisting of thousands of mourners threaded through the streets of Florence to the final resting places. Such ceremonies became a matter of civic importance to the city that could boast more great painters than any other. Fame, death, and working in Florence did not necessarily guarantee burial within the city's walls. Leonardo, for

A painting of Leonardo da Vinci on his deathbed attended by grief-stricken patrons including the king of France.

example, is buried in France and Raphael in Rome. Nonetheless, for some of the most celebrated Florentine painters, plaques and monuments pay final homage.

The importance of maintaining Florence's reputation as the leading city for the arts was well understood by prominent Florentine families. The city generated considerable revenues from tourists and art enthusiasts who came to the city not only to admire and purchase art but also to pay respect at the tombs of the dead masters. For this reason, the Medici family paid for many of the sculptured tombs and their inscriptions celebrating the lives of famous artists.

Some Florentine painters were so esteemed that when they were carried to their burial places, the entire city closed down as the funeral process wound through the streets. When Lippi died and was carried to the cemetery, Vasari remarked that "He was buried by his sons and while the funeral was passing, all the shops were closed, as is usually done for princes only."[102]

There are historical references to Giotto's funeral as well, describing thousands of people, both royalty and commoners, who expressed their appreciation for the greatest early Renaissance painter who began his life herding sheep and ended it in the great Cathedral of Florence with this epitaph:

> I am he through whose merit the lost art of painting was revived; whose hand was as faultless as it was compliant. What my art lacked, nature herself lacked; to none other was it given to paint more or better. . . . But what need is there for words? I am Giotto, and my name alone tells more than a lengthy ode. [103]

By the time Leonardo, Raphael, and Michelangelo—the last of the great late Renaissance masters—had died, the Renaissance itself had died along with them, giving way to new painters and new artistic styles. By that time, painters had moved far beyond the era of the early Renaissance painters who had struggled to elevate their paintings to the level of artistic expressions appreciated by all art connoisseurs.

Post Renaissance Florentine painters who walked the streets of the city and were recognized as important members of the city's rich intellectual tradition, understood that their status and good fortune was the result of the hard work and dedication of their predecessors.

NOTES

CHAPTER 1: THE EMERGENCE OF RENAISSANCE PAINTERS

1. Quoted in Francis Ames-Lewis, *The Intellectual Life of the Early Renaissance*. New Haven, CT: Yale University Press, 2000, p. 178.
2. Leon Battista Alberti, *On Painting*, trans. John R. Spencer. New Haven, CT: Yale University Press, 1970, p. 93.
3. Giorgio Vasari, *The Lives of the Artists*, ed. Betty Burroughs. New York: Simon & Schuster, 1946, p. 194.
4. Quoted in Vasari, *The Lives of the Artists*, p. 67.
5. Vasari, *The Lives of the Artists*, p. 301.
6. Vasari, *The Lives of the Artists*, p. 162.
7. Quoted in Ames-Lewis, *The Intellectual Life of the Early Renaissance*, p. 260.
8. Quoted in Ames-Lewis, *The Intellectual Life of the Early Renaissance*, p. 31.
9. Quoted in Ames-Lewis, *The Intellectual Life of the Early Renaissance*, p. 31.
10. Quoted in Vasari, *The Lives of the Artists*, p. 253.
11. Vasari, *The Lives of the Artists*, p. 253.
12. Cennino Cennini, *The Craftsman's Handbook*, trans. D.V. Thompson. New Haven, CT: Yale University Press, 1933, p. 15.
13. Quoted in Ames-Lewis, *The Intellectual Life of the Early Renaissance*, p. 274.
14. Quoted in Ames-Lewis, *The Intellectual Life of the Early Renaissance*, p. 275.
15. Quoted in Ames-Lewis, *The Intellectual Life of the Early Renaissance*, p. 275.
16. Quoted in Ames-Lewis, *The Intellectual Life of the Early Renaissance*, p. 1.
17. Quoted in Ames-Lewis, *The Intellectual Life of the Early Renaissance*, pp. 1–2.

CHAPTER 2: EDUCATION IN A *BOTTEGA*

18. Alberti, *On Painting*, p. 107.
19. Cennini, *The Craftsman's Handbook*, pp. 64–65.
20. Cennini, *The Craftsman's Handbook*, pp. 2–3.
21. Quoted in Vasari, *The Lives of the Artists*, p. 164.
22. Quoted in Vasari, *The Lives of the Artists*, p. 165.
23. Quoted in Vasari, *The Lives of the Artists*, p. 178.
24. Cennini, *The Craftsman's Handbook*, pp. 2–3.
25. Ascanio Condivi, *The Life of Michelangelo*, trans. Alice Sedgwick

Wohl. Baton Rouge: Louisiana State University Press, 1976, p. 9.

26. Vasari, *The Lives of the Artists,* p. 16.

27. Cennini, *The Craftsman's Handbook,* p. 3.

28. Cennini, *The Craftsman's Handbook,* p. 15.

29. Quoted in Creighton Gilbert, *Italian Art, 1400–1500: Sources and Documents.* Englewood Cliffs, NJ: Prentice-Hall, 1980, p. 156.

30. Vasari, *The Lives of the Artists,* pp. 192–93.

31. Quoted in Gilbert, *Italian Art, 1400–1500,* p. 43.

32. Quoted in D.S. Chambers, *Patrons and Artists in the Italian Renaissance.* London: Macmillan, 1970, p. 188.

33. Vasari, *The Lives of the Artists,* p. 232.

34. Quoted in Ames-Lewis, *The Intellectual Life of the Early Renaissance,* p. 30.

35. Quoted in Ames-Lewis, *The Intellectual Life of the Early Renaissance,* p. 31.

36. Cennini, *The Craftsman's Handbook,* p. 16.

37. Quoted in Gilbert, *Italian Art, 1400–1500,* p. 34.

38. Vasari, *The Lives of the Artists,* p. 53.

39. Cennini, *The Craftsman's Handbook,* p. 15.

40. Quoted in Gilbert, *Italian Art, 1400–1500,* p. 163.

41. Vasari, *The Lives of the Artists,* p. 191.

42. Martin Wackernagel, *The World of the Florentine Renaissance Artist,* trans. Alison Luchs. Princeton, NJ: Princeton University Press, 1981, p. 332.

43. Vasari, *The Lives of the Artists,* p. 194.

44. Cennini, *The Craftsman's Handbook,* p. 16.

45. Condivi, *The Life of Michelangelo,* p. 17.

46. Condivi, *The Life of Michelangelo,* p. 97.

CHAPTER 3: WORKING IN A *BOTTEGA*

47. Condivi, *The Life of Michelangelo,* p. 58.

48. Cennini, *The Craftsman's Handbook,* p. 27.

49. Cennini, *The Craftsman's Handbook,* p. 29.

50. Vasari, *The Lives of the Artists,* p. 80.

51. Condivi, *The Life of Michelangelo,* p. 10.

52. Vasari, *The Lives of the Artists,* p. 170.

53. Vasari, *The Lives of the Artists,* p. 259.

CHAPTER 4: WORKING OUTSIDE A *BOTTEGA*

54. Cennini, *The Craftsman's Handbook,* p. 42.

55. Michael Fuller, interview with the author, Berkeley, CA, April 28, 2002.
56. Vasari, *The Lives of the Artists,* p. 269.
57. Quoted in Vasari, *The Lives of the Artists,* p. 140.
58. Vasari, *The Lives of the Artists,* p. 196.
59. Quoted in Vasari, *The Lives of the Artists,* p. 166.
60. Vasari, *The Lives of the Artists,* p. 110.

CHAPTER 5: PATRONS AND PAINTERS

61. Vasari, *The Lives of the Artists,* p. 145.
62. Quoted in Vasari, *The Lives of the Artists,* p. 265.
63. Vasari, *The Lives of the Artists,* p. 267.
64. Quoted in Robert Klein, *Italian Art, 1500–1600: Sources and Documents.* Englewood Cliffs, NJ: Prentice Hall, 1966, pp. 161–62.
65. Quoted in Klein, *Italian Art, 1500–1600,* p. 132.
66. Vasari, *The Lives of the Artists,* p. 263.
67. Quoted in Klein, *Italian Art, 1500–1600,* p. 168.
68. Quoted in Vasari, *The Lives of the Artists,* p. 275.
69. Quoted in Wackernagel, *The World of the Florentine Renaissance Artist,* p. 208.
70. Quoted in Vasari, *The Lives of the Artists,* p. 139.

CHAPTER 6: ART AS A BUSINESS

71. Quoted in Ames-Lewis, *The Intellectual Life of the Early Renaissance,* p. 78.
72. Vasari, *The Lives of the Artists,* p. 190.
73. Quoted in Vasari, *The Lives of the Artists,* p. 207.
74. Quoted in Bruce Cole, *The Renaissance Artist at Work.* New York: Harper & Row, 1983, p. 54.
75. Quoted in Chambers, *Patrons and Artists in the Italian Renaissance,* p. 8.
76. Vasari, *The Lives of the Artists,* p. 229.
77. Vasari, *The Lives of the Artists,* p. 169.
78. Vasari, *The Lives of the Artists,* p. 169.
79. Vasari, *The Lives of the Artists,* p. 229.
80. Vasari, *The Lives of the Artists,* p. 268.
81. Quoted in Vasari, *The Lives of the Artists,* p. 67.
82. Vasari, *The Lives of the Artists,* p. 225.

CHAPTER 7: THE PRIVATE LIVES AND PERSONALITIES OF FLORENTINE PAINTERS

83. Vasari, *The Lives of the Artists,* p. 147.
84. Vasari, *The Lives of the Artists,* p. 167.
85. Vasari, *The Lives of the Artists,* p. 229.

86. Vasari, *The Lives of the Artists,* p. 294.

87. Vasari, *The Lives of the Artists,* p. 295.

88. Quoted in Vasari, *The Lives of the Artists,* p. 18.

89. Quoted in Vasari, *The Lives of the Artists,* p. 197.

90. Quoted in Klein, *Italian Art, 1500–1600,* p. 165.

91. Vasari, *The Lives of the Artists,* p. 209.

92. Quoted in Wackernagel, *The World of the Florentine Renaissance Artist,* p. 358.

93. Vasari, *The Lives of the Artists,* p. 188.

94. Vasari, *The Lives of the Artists,* p. 206.

95. Vasari, *The Lives of the Artists,* p. 192.

96. Quoted in Vasari, *The Lives of the Artists,* p. 19.

97. Wackernagel, *The World of the Florentine Renaissance Artist,* p. 352.

98. Quoted in Wackernagel, *The World of the Florentine Renaissance Artist,* p. 353.

99. Quoted in Klein, *Italian Art, 1500–1600,* p. 59.

100. Quoted in Vasari, *The Lives of the Artists,* p. 58.

101. Quoted in, Gilbert, *Italian Art, 1400–1500,* p. 157.

102. Vasari, *The Lives of the Artists,* p. 163.

103. Quoted in Sarel Eimerl, *The World of Giotto.* New York: Time-Life Publishers, 1978, p. 7.

FOR FURTHER READING

Anita Albus, *The Art of Arts: Rediscovering Painting*. Trans. Michael Robertson. Berkeley: University of California Press, 2000. Albus presents photographs of hundreds of world-famous paintings, including brief descriptions of each. The author draws the reader into the world of the painting by presenting her views on color, perspective, and Renaissance symbolism.

James Barter, *Artists of the Renaissance*. San Diego, CA: Lucent Books, 1999. Barter presents the lives and accomplishments of six painters, sculptors, and architects who represent the early and high Renaissance: Giotto, Donatello, Brunelleschi, Leonardo, Michelangelo, and Raphael. The works and lives of these artisans are presented within the historical context of the Renaissance.

David Alan Brown, *Leonardo da Vinci: Origins of a Genius*. New Haven, CT: Yale University Press, 1988. This book is the first full-length study of Leonardo's beginnings as an artist. It discusses his years as an apprentice in Verrocchio's workshop and his subsequent work on his own, the development of his technique, and the relationship of his early paintings to each other and to their sources.

Serafina Hager, *Leonardo, Michelangelo, and Raphael in Renaissance Florence from 1500 to 1508*. Washington, DC: Georgetown University Press, 1992. The few years when these three masters of the late Renaissance resided in Florence was a remarkable time for Western art. Hager writes a compelling history of the three men, their art, and their quarrels. This book is interesting for its discussions of paintings as well as its history.

Pierluigi de Vecchi, *Michelangelo: The Vatican Frescoes*. New York: Abbeville Press, 1997. This book presents a history of the Sistine Chapel in its entirety, from the Creation to the Last Judgment. In addition to excellent text, the book includes 250 color photographs of the frescoes before and after the restoration.

WORKS CONSULTED

Leon Battista Alberti, *On Painting.* Trans. John R. Spencer. New Haven, CT: Yale University Press, 1970. Alberti's book was the first book written by a painter to provide instruction to younger painters. It is organized into three chapters covering the importance of learning the geometry of perspective, the study of the ancient masters, and the rendering of various subjects.

Francis Ames-Lewis, *The Intellectual Life of the Early Renaissance.* New Haven, CT: Yale University Press, 2000. Ames-Lewis explores the ways in which painters and sculptors of the early Renaissance raised intellectual questions while they sought to elevate the craft of painting to a liberal art form. Ames-Lewis makes the point that it was over this period that the idea of the artist as a creative genius with an individual identity surfaced.

Cennino Cennini, *The Craftsman's Handbook.* Trans. D.V. Thompson. New Haven, CT: Yale University Press, 1933. Cennini wrote this handbook as a primer for painters to instruct them in the practical arts of painting. The book covers hundreds of topics, from advice on selecting a master painter to making paints and paintbrushes to painting frescoes.

D.S. Chambers, *Patrons and Artists in the Italian Renaissance.* London: Macmillan, 1970. Chambers provides an in-depth analysis of the interdependence between artists and patrons, focusing on the wealthy aristocracy and the higher offices of the Catholic Church that paid for the majority of Renaissance masterpieces.

Bruce Cole, *The Renaissance Artist at Work.* New York: Harper & Row, 1983. Cole provides excellent insight into the world and lives of Renaissance artists as they went about their jobs. The book provides detailed information on many fascinating topics such as artists' place in society, their training, patrons, and the materials they used to execute their works.

Ascanio Condivi, *The Life of Michelangelo.* Trans. Alice Sedgwick Wohl. Baton Rouge: Louisiana State University Press, 1976. Condivi was the official biographer of Michelangelo. A personal friend, Condivi asked Michelangelo to review his book and edit it where he felt it needed clarification. This book became the source for most of Vasari's comments on Michelangelo and is therefore considered the source for much of what is known about the master artist.

Sarel Eimerl, *The World of Giotto,* New York: Time-Life Publishers, 1978. True to all other books in this series, Great Painters, this one provides an excellent and broad discussion of Giotto's life and his paintings that elevated him to the pinnacle of early Renaissance art. In addition to clear discussions of why Giotto is revered today are well-chosen high-quality photos of Giotto's paintings.

Creighton Gilbert, *Italian Art, 1400–1500: Sources and Documents.* Englewood Cliffs, NJ: Prentice-Hall, 1980. This is a collection of historically interesting documents covering the middle Renaissance. All documents are letters, contracts, or legal decisions regarding artists and their patrons.

Craig Harbison, *The Mirror of the Artist.* New York: Harry N. Abrams, 1995. Harbison, who is a professor of art history, examines the state of mind and the cultural moment that produced the superlative art of the fifteenth and sixteenth centuries. The book is well documented and well illustrated.

Robert Klein, *Italian Art, 1500–1600: Sources and Documents.* Englewood Cliffs, NJ: Prentice Hall, 1966. This is a collection of historically interesting documents covering the late Renaissance. All documents are letters, contracts, or legal decisions regarding artists and their patrons.

Giorgio Vasari, *The Lives of the Artists.* Ed. Betty Burroughs. New York: Simon & Schuster, 1946. Vasari's collection of biographies of nearly thirty Renaissance artists is the finest collection of source material available for understanding these masters. Although Vasari is at times overly complimentary about his subjects, each biography is a gem for Renaissance scholars.

Martin Wackernagel, *The World of the Florentine Renaissance Artist.* Trans. Alison Luchs. Princeton, NJ: Princeton University Press, 1981. Martin Wackernagel has written a remarkable comprehensive book about the Renaissance artists between 1420 and 1530. He focuses on the economic, social, and commercial activities of artists, their patrons, and business practices between the two groups.

INDEX

Alberti, Leon Battista
  academics for apprentices and, 30
  on artists' training, 22
  Cosimo de Medici and, 69
  fabricated models and, 36
  on imitating nature, 14
  marriage and, 50
  on perspective, 17
Albertini, Francesco, 25
Angelico, 19, 69
Apelles (Greek artist), 92
apprentices, 11–12
  academics an, 29–31
  accurate rendering of dress by,
    32–33
  architecture and, 31–32
  copying of masters by, 31–33
  finding a master, 26–29
  first year for, 42
  gathering of pigments by, 42–43
  grinding of pigments by, 44–45
  master painters role in, 22–24
  older, 46–49
  parents and, 25–26
  study of human anatomy and,
    33–37
  use of fabricated models by, 36
  use of live models for, 34
  work done by, 41–45
Arena Chapel, 51
Aretino, Pietro, 88
Armenini, G.B.
  on aristocratic patron's requests, 65

art business, 72–84
  bottega as a gallery, 47
  three types of patrons in, 60
artists
  animosity between, 88
  business acumen of, 84
  compliments of each other, 94
  constructive criticism and, 92
  contracts and commissions and,
    77–79
  contributions to by assistants,
    79–82
  cost of commissions by, 60
  dress of, 56
  eccentric behavior of, 89–91
  families and, 50
  gifts to wealthy collectors by, 74,
    76
  humor and, 91, 93
  posthumous honors of, 94–96
  salaries of, 75
  schooling of, 22–37
  social acceptability of, 20–21
  spending habits of, 85–88
  techniques of
    chiaroscuro, 15
    creating pigments and paints,
      42–45
    illusion of mist or smoke, 32
    imitation of nature and, 12–15
    individual styles and, 18–20
    making of paint brushes, 41
    painting of frescoes and, 52, 54

perspective, 15–18
use of gold leaf, 81
verbal confrontations between, 93–94

Bartolommeo, 32
alternative to live models, 36
as a master, 29
Barzizza, Gasparino
on copying masters' art, 31
Basilica of San Lorenzo, 69
Bicci, Neri di, 28
Boniface VIII (pope), 89
Botticelli, Sandro, 76, 94
fortune of, 85–86
marriage and, 50
style of, 19
Bramante, 62
Brunelleschi, Filippo
as architect, 31
Cosimo de Medici and, 69
guilds and, 73
perspective and, 15, 18
Buonarotti, Michelangelo. *See* Michaelangelo

Calumny of Apelles (Botticelli), 76
Campanile (Giotto's Bell Tower), 32
Castagno, Andrea del, 88
Cathedral of Florence, 96
Catholic Church, 12
as art patron, 60–65
censorship of art and, 64–66
Mantegna and, 74, 76
success of artists and, 85
Cennini, Cennino
apprentices and, 22–23, 26

mathematics and, 30–31
motivations of, 24–25
on copying the masters, 31
on creating black paint, 44
on imitating nature, 13–14
individual style of, 18–19
on making paintbrushes, 41
on painting as a gentleman's job, 56
on painting frescoes, 52
on use of fabricated models, 36
Chigi, Agostino, 59
Cimabue, 26, 45
Condivi, Ascanio
on Michelangelo and his father, 25–26
on Michelangelo's reluctance to do the Sistine Chapel, 63
on Michelangelo's use of cadavers, 36–37
on relationships between artists, 88
Cosimo, Piero di, 77
bizarre behavior of, 91
eating habits of, 90
marriage and, 50
Cossa, Francesco del, 77
Currado, David di Tommaso di, 28
Craftsman's Handbook, The (Cennini), 13, 25, 41, 44, 56

Delli, Dello, 56
d'Esti, Isabella, 20
Donatello, 69, 94
Doni, Agnolo, 65
Duchess Beatrice, 66
Duke Alfonso, 67
Duke Ludovico, 66

Dürer, Albrecht, 17

Fabro, del Pippo, 34
Filarete
  on models for artists, 32
Filippo, Filippino di, 94
Flood, The (Michelangelo), 63
Florence, Italy, 10, 68
  aristocracy in, 66
  art guide to, 25
  as artists' training ground, 24–26
  as capital of Renaissance art, 68
  districts and structure of, 27
  reasons to apprentice in, 24
  vacationers and, 12
France, 20
frescoes
  costliness of, 75
  difficulty of painting, 52
  emotional strain on painters and,
    57–59
  geometry of, 53
  as highest calling for painter,
    51–52
  master painters and, 48–49
  preliminary sketches for, 47–48
  preparing the wall for, 55, 57
  process of painting, 52, 54
  use of scaffolding for, 54–55
Fuller, Michael
  on painting a fresco, 54

Gates of Paradise (Ghilberti), 32
Ghiberti, Lorenzo, 69
  academics and, 29–30
Ghirlandaio, Domenico di, 10, 94
Gilbert, Creighton

on depicting clothing, 32
on Francesco del Cossa, 77
Giotto di Bonde, 10, 26
  as an apprentice, 45
  Arena Chapel and, 51
  building of, drawn by apprentices,
    31–32
  fresh ideas by, 78
  funeral of, 95–96
  marriage and, 50
  sense of humor and, 93
  superior skills of, 89
Giovanni, Matteo di, 78
  as Michelangelo's master, 28, 49
  middle class and, 70–71
  poor treatment of, while working
    on fresco, 55
  wages of, 75
  workshop of, 39–42
Giovanni Santi
  poem about artists, 20
guilds, 68, 72–74

Holy Tribunal, 65
House of Medici, 69

Italian Art, 1400–1500 (Gilbert), 32,
  77
Italian Art 1500–1600 (Klein), 88

Julius II (pope), 62–63

Klein, Robert
  on Arentino and Michelangelo, 88

La Fornarina (Raphael), 58
Last Judgement, The (Michelangelo), 88

Last Supper (Leonardo), 53
Last Supper
  Veronese's depiction of, 64–65
Leda and the Swan (Michelangelo),
  67
Leo (pope), 55, 57
Leoanrdo da Vinci, 10, 76
  academics studied by apprentices
    and, 30
  bragging of, 89
  burial of, 94–95
  creating balanced design in paint-
    ing and, 32
  custom scaffolding made by, 54–55
  drawing of Neptune by, 76
  faithful reproduction of Mona
    Lisa's face by, 14
  fast horses and, 86
  geometry and, 53
  enmity toward Raphael by, 88
  on lack of originality by painters, 82
  marriage and, 50
  painting of shield by, 76
  passion for rendering faces, 33
  preparing wall for painting, 55, 57
  sense of humor and, 93
  sitting of Mona Lisa and, 34–35
  social status of, 20–21
  study of anatomy and, 30
  tribute to Masaccio's ability to
    copy nature, 14
  use of aristocrats faces in paintings
    by, 66
  Vasari and, 16
  work on perspective by, 17
Life of Michelangelo, The (Condivi),
  63

Lippi, Fra Filippo
  funeral of, 95
  realism and, 15
  womanizing and, 59
Lives of the Artists, The (Vasari), 16,
  88

Mantegna, Andrea
  gift to bishop from, 74, 76
  style of painting and, 20
  visit by Lorenzo Medici, 47
Masaccio (Tommasso of Florence),
  82, 86–87
  ability to copy nature, 14
  fight with Torrigiano, 45–46
  Giovanni de Medici and, 69
  marriage and, 50
  preferred dress of, 56
  style of, 19
  use of perspective by, 18
Medici e Speziali (guild), 72
Medici, Cosimo de, 59, 69
Medici, Giovanni de, 69
Medici, Lorenzo de, 69
Medici, Lorenzo de "the
  Magnificent," 66, 69
  as art patron, 47
Medici, Piero de, 67, 69
  lack of respect for artists, 65
Medici family
  sculptured tombs for artists, 95
Michelangelo, 10, 66, 69
  Agnolo Doni and, 64
  artistic skills of, 49
  bohemian lifestyle of, 87–88
  employment of apprentices and,
    28, 82

fall from scaffolding, 55
guilds and, 73, 79
marriage and, 50
personal arrogance of, 89
Piero de Medici and, 65
preferred dress of, 56
Raphael and, 82–83, 93–94
relationship with father and, 25–26
Sistine Chapel and, 52, 57, 62–63, 75
social standing of, 21
use of cadavers by, 36–37
use of perspective by, 17–18
Visari and, 16
worked on Via Ghibellina, 38
work for the church, 60
Middle Ages, 18
Mirandola, Giovanni Pico della, 69
Mona Lisa (*La Gioconda*) , 35–36
faithful reproduction of, 14
Moses (Michelangelo), 62

Nude Diana (Titian), 17

Old Marketplace (Mercato Vecchio), 43
On Painting (Alberti), 14, 22, 92

Palazzo Caprini, "House of Raphael," 86
Paradise (Angelico), 19
Passignano (abbey), 55
aristocratic, 65– 67, 85
at the bottega, 47
middle classes, 69–71
vacationers as, 12
see also Catholic Church

Perseus Liberating Andromeda (Cosimo), 91
Perugino
elegant houses and, 86
as a master of frescos, 24
obtaining pigment by, 57
on reasons to go to Florence, 94
Pino, Paolo
on verbal sparing of artists, 94
Pinturicchio, Bernardino, 49
use of apprentices to complete paintings, 80–81
Pisa, Italy, 68
Pius II (pope), 81
Pollaiuolo, Antonio, 60

Quercia, Jacopo della, 78

Raphael of Urbino, 10
arrogance of, 89
assistants and, 79–82
burial of, 95
cartoons for pope's library and, 81
enmity with Leonardo, 88
marriage and, 50
as a master, 28–29
Michelangelo and, 63, 82, 89, 93–94
patrons and, 58
Pope Julius and, 62
use of light and dark and, 15
Vasari and, 16
villa in Rome of, 86
women and, 86
Reniassance
economy of, 12

end of, 96
time of, 10
Robert (king of Naples), 93
Rome, Italy, 68
Rosselli, Cosimo
  contract with master for, 28

Saint Philip, 15
San Agostino, 82
San Gallo, 63
San Gimignano (town), 55
San Petronio, 78
Sansovino, Jacopo, 34
Santa Maria del Fiore, 32
Santa Maria delle Grazi (Milan)
  Last Supper painted at, 53
Santo Spirito, 68
Savonarola (monk), 27
School of Athens, The (Raphael), 80,
  89, 90
Scrovegni family, 51
Segni, Antonio, 76
Sforza, Ludovico, 89
Siena (Italy), 81
Signorelli, Luca, 24
Sistine Chapel, 93
  amount of time to paint, 52
  Michelangelo's feelings of impris-
    onment in, 62–63
  Michelangelo's wages for, 75
  use of assistants on, 82
Sodoma, Il
  love of animals by, 91
Squarcione, Francesco
  teaching of geometry and, 31
St. Barbara Enthroned (Giovanni),
  78, 79

St. Catherine the German, 78
St. Mary Magdalene, 78
Strozzi Chapel, 15
St. Sebastian, 74
Souvenir of Many Statues and
  Paintings in the City of Florence, A
  (Albertini), 25

Titian, 17
Torrigiano, Pietro, 45–46
Two Cripples (Masaccio), 19

Uccello, Paolo, 18, 69, 94
University of California (Berkeley),
  54

Vasari, Giorgio, 92
  academics for apprentices and, 31
  art history and, 16
  comment on Raphael's use of light
    and dark, 15
  on Dello Delli's dress, 56
  on Giotto as an apprentice, 45, 46
  on Leonardo
    exotic birds, 91
    facial renderings, 33
    commission from Pope Leo, 55,
    57
  on Michelangelo
    grinding own pigments, 42
    difficulties at Sistine Chapel, 55
  on perfection of Mona Lisa, 14
  on Perugino and great houses, 86
  on Raphael as a master, 28–29
  on relationships between artists, 88
  on working for the church, 60–61
Vatican (Rome), 57

Venice, Italy, 68
Veronese, Paolo
  deviation from church's standard
    by, 64–65
Verrocchio
  marriage and, 50
Vespignano, 26
Via Ghibellina, 38

Via Tosconella, 38
Vitruvian Man (Leonardo), 30

Wackernagel, Martin
  on artists' malicious tongues, 93
  on use of live models, 34
Wedding of Cana, The (Veronese),
  64

PICTURE CREDITS

James Barter is the author of more than a dozen nonfiction books for middle school students. He received his undergraduate degree in history and classics at the University of California Berkeley followed by graduate studies in ancient history and archaeology at the University of Pennsylvania. Barter has taught history as well as Latin and Greek.

A Fulbright scholar at the American Academy in Rome, Barter worked on archaeological sites in and around the city as well as on sites in the Naples area. He also has worked and traveled extensively in Greece.

Barter currently lives in Rancho Santa Fe, California, with his seventeen-year-old daughter, Kalista.